PEACE,
be STILL

PEACE,
be STILL

DAVID S. BAXTER

CFI
An imprint of Cedar Fort, Inc.
Springville, Utah

ISBN 13: 978-1-4621-1340-8

Published by CFI, an imprint of Cedar Fort, Inc.
2373 W. 700 S., Springville, UT 84663
Distributed by Cedar Fort, Inc., www.cedarfort.com

LIBRARY OF CONGRESS CATALOGING-IN-PUBLICATION DATA

Baxter, David S. (David Steward), 1955- author.
Peace, be still / David S. Baxter.
    pages cm
Includes bibliographical references.
ISBN 978-1-4621-1340-8 (alk. paper)
1. Peace--Religious aspects--Church of Jesus Christ of Latter-day Saints. 2. Church of Jesus Christ of Latter-day Saints--Doctrines. I. Title.

BX8643.P43B39 2013
242--dc23

2013023176

Cover design by Shawnda T. Craig
Cover design © 2013 Lyle Mortimer
Typeset by Michelle May
Edited by Valene Wood and Emily Chambers

Printed in the United States of America

10 9 8 7 6 5 4 3 2 1

Printed on acid-free paper

To my eternal companion, Dianne,
who has always been the epitome of peaceful serenity.

Contents

Preface

*I*t seems to me that we have increasingly created life conditions in a world in which it is difficult to simply "be still." Instead, we have a world that is furiously fast, balefully busy, and numbingly noisy. We barely have a moment to spare; every minute has to be filled with something—anything.

Even Sundays can be busy, busy, busy. Supermarket parking lots are full, and stores are bursting with customers. Long ago, Sunday was regarded by many as the Sabbath; now it is not even a day of rest for most people.

In these pages I set out aspects of "peace" for individuals, families, communities, and nations. These concepts may be considered overly ideal, but they are not meant to be perfect, ubiquitous, or all-embracing. They are simply reflections and observations. I invite each reader to ponder them, even using them as something of a "barometer check" to determine which ways the winds of life are blowing, and if we will be happy with their current trajectory, direction, and destination. Is our personal world bringing peace or turmoil?

A fundamental focus—an intrinsic purpose—is to encourage introspective insight, reflection, and revelation. It is not my intent to be dogmatic, prescriptive, or to tell people what to do.

My own hope is that the contents of this book will enable every reader to identify, feel, and realize a greater sense of personal peace and find out how to obtain, to a degree at least, some moments of personal pause from the debilitating, suffocating stress of life—to enjoy some serene stillness in the midst of cacophonous commotion.

Although I serve in a leadership position in The Church of Jesus Christ of Latter-day Saints, (hereafter referred to as "the Church"), the contents and views expressed are entirely my own. They do not represent the views, opinions, or positions of the Church or its leadership, nor is it intended that they should do so. This is entirely my own work, and I alone am responsible for its contents and positions, faults and all.

I remain eternally grateful to my wife, Dianne, who in every circumstance of life has been calm, peaceful, and quietly reassuring.

I am indebted to Alice Ann Weber, who has typed and retyped this manuscript.

—David Baxter

Prologue

1. Master, the tempest is raging!
The billows are tossing high!
The sky is o'ershadowed with blackness.
No shelter or help is nigh.
Carest thou not that we perish?
How canst thou lie asleep
When each moment so madly is threat'ning
A grave in the angry deep?

[Chorus]
The winds and the waves shall obey thy will:
Peace, be still.
Whether the wrath of the storm-tossed sea
Or demons or men or whatever it be,
No waters can swallow the ship where lies
The Master of ocean and earth and skies.
They all shall sweetly obey thy will:
Peace, be still; peace, be still.
They all shall sweetly obey thy will:
Peace, peace, be still.

2. Master, with anguish of spirit
I bow in my grief today.
The depths of my sad heart are troubled.

Oh, waken and save, I pray!
Torrents of sin and of anguish
Sweep o'er my sinking soul,
And I perish! I perish! dear Master.
Oh, hasten and take control!

3. Master, the terror is over.
The elements sweetly rest.
Earth's sun in the calm lake is mirrored,
And heaven's within my breast.
Linger, O blessed Redeemer!
Leave me alone no more,
And with joy I shall make the blest harbor
And rest on the blissful shore.

Hymns, "Master, the Tempest Is Raging," no. 105

CHAPTER 1

The Still, Small Voice

*P*erpetual peace comes through the instrumentality of the Holy Ghost. The Holy Ghost, the third member of the Godhead, is the harbinger, the messenger of peace. Through His "still, small voice" we are prompted, comforted, encouraged, and elevated. Although those of other faiths, and those who have none, can be and are touched by the Holy Ghost, it is to members of the Church who have been baptized and confirmed that the opportunity has come to "receive" the divine gift of the Holy Ghost. It is an entitlement, a blessing from heaven, insofar as the individuals live so as to merit the gift. If he or she does, then the soul-satisfying entitlement includes an ongoing witness of the truth, the blessing of the Holy Spirit of Promise, consoling comfort, confirmation and guidance, and perfect stillness.

An Ongoing Witness of the Truth

As Jesus promised His apostles, "when the comforter is come, whom I will send unto you from the Father, even the spirit of truth, which proceedeth from the Father, he shall testify of me" (John 15:26).

This is a primary role of the Holy Ghost. He testifies of Heavenly Father and of Jesus Christ. In this promise, as ever, Jesus is careful to acknowledge the Father; He makes clear that the Holy Ghost comes from the Father, and that one of His roles is to testify of the Savior, and by definition, all of the aspects of the doctrine of Christ, the gospel of Christ—of His ways, teachings, commandments, His atoning mission, of His reality and central role in Heavenly Father's plan.

It is particularly significant that this promise was at first directed to the Apostles, the men who were to represent Him in all the world. It is through the Holy Ghost that such a penetrating witness comes. When one is filled with the power of the Holy Ghost, when one receives a deep penetrating and all-inclusive manifestation of the Holy Ghost, one's view of life completely changes; the individual witness of Jesus Christ and all of His ways is pervasive, totally enveloping, and inspiring.

I venture to suggest that such a witness from the Holy Ghost is even more pervasive and enduring than a personal visitation from the Savior. After all, the original Twelve Apostles walked and talked daily with the Savior, sat at His feet, touched Him, and were touched by Him. They travelled with Him, broke bread with Him, even had their feet washed by Him. Yet one betrayed Him, one denied Him, one doubted the reality of the Resurrection, all were to murmur at the Last Supper wondering which of them was the greatest, and all had the experience of not being able to heal the lunatic son of a man who eventually came to Jesus for the miracle that he sought in faith.

The man said, "I brought him to thy disciples, and they could not cure him" (Matthew 17:16). The Savior rebuked the devil, and the young man was healed. The disciples were left to ask, "Why could not we cast him out?" (Matthew 17:19).

Though they walked and talked with the Savior, these ordinary men did not yet have absolute faith, loyalty, or power. Yet it was these same men of whom we read in the rest of the New Testament who performed many miracles and taught with great power and authority on hilltops, in towns and villages, and before kings and rulers. Primarily, they received as promised the powerful witness of the Holy Spirit—the Holy Ghost. We read in the book of Acts that, on the day of Pentecost when the Apostles "were all with one accord in one place. And suddenly there came a sound from heaven . . . and it filled all the house where they were sitting. . . . And they were all filled with the Holy Ghost" (Acts 2:1–4).

So great was this spiritual witness that Peter, who had denied knowing Jesus just a short time before, "standing up with the eleven, lifted up his voice to [a multitude], and said unto them, Ye men of Judea, all ye that dwell at Jerusalem, be this known unto you, and hearken to my words" (Acts 2:14).

There then followed from the lips of Peter one of the most powerful witnesses of the Savior, the Holy Ghost, and the gospel that perhaps has ever been given, as well as this precious invitation for the ages: "repent, and be baptized every one of you in the name of Jesus Christ for the remission of sins, and ye shall receive the gift of the Holy Ghost" (Acts 2:38). So powerful was this witness that three thousand people were baptized that very day. Receipt of the divine gift of the Holy Ghost made all the difference to these servants of the Lord, as it can do for each of us.

Later, after their miraculous escape from prison, Peter and John were able to testify to the priests, "we are his witnesses of these things; and so is also the Holy Ghost whom God hath given to them that obey him" (Acts 5:32).

This powerful manifestation of the Holy Ghost was not exclusive to the Twelve. We read in Acts that seven others were called, including Stephen who was to be martyred, to assist the Twelve. There were "seven men of honest report, full of the Holy Ghost and wisdom, whom we may appoint over this business" (Acts 6:3).

So it is in the Church today, the Twelve Apostles, who serve as living witnesses of Jesus Christ and all of His works, and the Seventy, who have been called to assist them in the work. As we read in modern revelation: "The Twelve Apostles, or special witnesses of the name of Christ in all the world . . . [are to be aided in the work by] the Seventy, [who] are also called to preach the gospel, and to be especial witnesses unto the Gentiles and in all the world" (Doctrine & Covenants 107:23, 25). Further, that the Twelve are "to call upon the Seventy, when they need assistance, . . . instead of any others" (Doctrine & Covenants 107:38).

The pattern, which was established in the New Testament Church, can be found today in The Church of Jesus Christ of Latter-day Saints. Although one of the least of men, I have nevertheless been called and ordained as one of the Seventy in modern times. Having been filled with the Holy Ghost, I am an "especial witness" of the "name of Jesus Christ in all the world." I know that Jesus Christ lives and is the Savior and Redeemer of all mankind. I can say that I know Him, because I have received that manifestation of the Holy Ghost.

A testimony of the power and truthfulness of the gospel in its fulness is available to every member of the Church. Confirmation following baptism makes that divine gift possible; but a price has to be paid for it.

President Joseph Fielding Smith stated:

The Holy Ghost will not dwell in unclean tabernacles or disobedient tabernacles. The Holy Ghost will not dwell with that person who is unwilling to obey and keep the commandments of God or who violates those commandments willfully. In such a soul the spirit of the Holy Ghost cannot enter.

That great gift comes to us only through humility and faith and obedience. . . . and without the guidance which is promised to us through our faithfulness, people are unable to discern and are led astray. It depends on our faithfulness and our obedience to the commandments of the Lord if we have the teachings, the enlightening instruction that comes from the Holy Ghost.[1]

To live so as to receive the constant companionship of the Holy Ghost is a price worth paying. It is a remarkable and wondrous thing to be entitled to this heavenly endowment of the complete and permanent companionship of the third member of the Godhead. Think of that! Is this not a superlative gift and honor?

We know that the things of God have to be "spiritually discerned," and that "the natural man receiveth not the things of the Spirit of God" (1 Corinthians 2:14). We also have this testimony of Paul: "Now we have received, not the spirit of the world, but the spirit which is of God; that we might know the things that are freely given to us of God" (1 Corinthians 2:12). Note that Paul does not say "believe," but that we might "know." Each of us may "know" of the doctrines and truthfulness of the gospel for ourselves through the enlightenment that comes from the Holy Ghost.

Of course, the Holy Ghost does not just shed forth in bearing witness of *eternal* truths—He is the revealer of *all* truth. It is my view that the greatest inventions and advancements in the world, including development of medical procedures and knowledge, have had their genesis in the revelation and inspiration from the Holy Ghost. While mortal men claim the astonishing advancements for themselves—their own genius as it were—the reality is that the "still, small voice" has been at work.

Scientists, academes, inventors, and other pioneers of thought and technology may have received Nobel prizes for their work, but that is only their side of the story. Of course, there is human genius and even brilliance, but the glory rightly belongs to the Holy Ghost acting on behalf of the Father. When I first laid my head in an MRI machine, saw the brain image, and obtained surgery to remove two brain tumors, I was somewhat amazed by the wonder of it all. I thought to myself how incredible this all was. How on earth did anyone conceive of such technology let alone construct it and make it all work? The truth is that men on earth did not conceive, invent, or produce such incredible technology and skill in and of themselves; it all came from the divine, heavenly source we know as the Holy Ghost, or the Light of Christ.

The Blessing of the Holy Spirit of Promise

The role of the Holy Ghost as the Holy Spirit of Promise is seldom referred to. It is, nevertheless, a most significant responsibility, to ratify all priesthood ordinances. President Joseph Fielding Smith explained, "The Holy Spirit of Promise is the Holy Ghost who places the stamp of approval upon every ordinance: baptism, confirmation, ordination, marriage. The promise is that the blessings will be received through faithfulness."[2] The Holy Spirit withdraws the stamp of approval where covenants are broken. Transgression will break any seal.

President Joseph Fielding Smith stated that, "every covenant, contract, bond, obligation, oath, vow, and performance that man receives through the covenants and blessings of the gospel, is sealed by the Holy Spirit of Promise. The promise is that the blessing will be obtained, if those who seek it are true and faithful to the end. If they are not faithful, then the Holy Spirit will withdraw the blessing, and the promise comes to an end."[3]

In other words, every commandment and covenant of the gospel has a blessing associated with it; for example, the blessings promised to those who obey the Word of Wisdom (see Doctrine & Covenants 89:18–21) and to those who live the Law of Tithing (See Malachi 3:10–11, and Doctrine & Covenants 64:23).

Unless we are faithful, the Holy Ghost—or Holy Spirit—will not ratify the promised blessings, which will then not be available. It is not the making of the covenant that brings the blessing, but the keeping of it. Then, the Holy Spirit of Promise confirms the blessing, and we receive it.

There is a sweet peace that flows from the keeping of covenants and obedience to the commandments as the Holy Ghost then provides confirmation of the associated blessings.

President Heber J. Grant noted, "No obstacles are insurmountable when God commands and we obey."[4]

The Holy Ghost prepares the way, clears the way, and confers the blessings.

Consoling Comfort

As well as declaring that the Holy Ghost would "testify of me," the Savior also promised, "the Comforter, which is the Holy Ghost, whom the Father will send in my name, he shall teach you all things, and bring all things to your remembrance, whatsoever I have said unto you. Peace I leave with you, my peace I give unto you. Let not your heart be troubled, neither let it be afraid" (John 14:26–27).

There we have it. The Holy Ghost brings comfort, and through Him the Savior brings peace.

Elder George Q. Cannon said, "Whenever darkness fills our minds, we may know that we are not possessed of the Spirit of God, and we must get rid of it. When we are filled with the Spirit of God, we are filled with joy, with peace, and with happiness no matter what our circumstances may be; for it is a spirit of cheerfulness and of happiness."[5]

In speaking of the Lord's promise of peace, President Marion G. Romney said, "There is no way to discourage or defeat a people or one person who follows the guidance of the Holy Spirit."[6]

In the aftermath of brain surgery, and in the midst of melancholy brought on by fear, uncertainty, and a sense of loss, I felt the consoling comfort of the Holy Ghost. It was not dramatic, nor was it a single event. Although it was not an easy experience, I simply spent many midnight hours on my knees, praying for help, often weeping for it. As this went on, I was increasingly blessed with a sense of spiritual peace and understanding. Although not immediately physically blessed, I nevertheless began to feel that I was being lifted up by the Savior, embraced by Him, "encircled about eternally in the arms of his love" (2 Nephi 1:15). This was the Holy Ghost. What a gift! What a blessing!

When we are in our extremity, feeling alone, sad, or fearful, the Holy Ghost can fill us with an almost overwhelming sense of love, goodness, and peace if we earnestly seek such comfort and consolation.

Confirmation and Guidance

It has been said that we cannot go wrong, cannot make a mistake, without the Holy Ghost warning us in advance. President Marion G.

Romney taught, "Now, I tell you that you can make every decision in your life correctly if you can learn to follow the guidance of the Holy Spirit. This you can do if you will discipline yourself to yield your own feelings to the promptings of the Spirit."[7]

On many occasions I have heard President Thomas S. Monson say, "Never ignore a prompting." It is good advice. It is my observation that if we ignore promptings of the Holy Ghost, there will come a time when promptings will cease. Promptings come as penetrating thoughts, impressions on our mind that suggest some course of action, usually in relation to what we can do for others. Some may consider such promptings to be no more than flights of fancy or simply the workings of our own mind, but over time we can come to discern those thoughts that invite us to do good as the promptings they truly are.

In the Book of Mormon, we read Alma's witness that "whatsoever is good cometh from God" (Alma 5:40). Later in the Book of Mormon we are taught, "And whatsoever thing persuadeth men to do good is of me . . . I am the same that leadeth men to all good. . . . I am the light, and the life, and the truth of the world" (Ether 4:12).

The teaching is clear. If we are prompted to do something good, we can be assured it comes from the Savior and is being communicated through the Holy Ghost, or the Light of Christ.

I know of one good priesthood leader who felt a strong impression to visit the home of a member but did not know the reason. Despite this lack of understanding, he just went to the home of this good brother. When the door was opened, the priesthood leader simply said, "Why am I here?" It became clear that there was severe family difficulty, and the priesthood leader was able to give counsel and comfort.

I also know of a sweet, humble sister who was serving as Relief Society president of our ward in England. In those days very few families owned cars, and we simply travelled everywhere using public transport. On this particular day, the good sister had been to the supermarket to buy groceries for her family. On the way home, and still some distance from her destination, she felt prompted to get off the bus and visit another sister; help was needed. She got off the bus, shopping bags and all, and made her way to the member's home. She discovered that the sister had fallen through a glass door, could not get up, and was badly injured. The timely intervention brought the medical help that was needed—and a life was saved.

Not all of our promptings are as dramatic as these, but whether they be large or small, every act that is prompted by the Holy Ghost is of great significance. Elder George Q. Cannon taught,

> It requires the utmost care upon the part of the people who have received the Spirit of the Lord by the laying on of hands to distinguish between the voice of that Spirit, and the voice of their own hearts . . . Experience and watchfulness will enable the Saint to recognize the voice of the Holy Spirit.
>
> It is a still, small voice . . . It is not boisterous, loud or aggressive, and if those who receive it carefully watch its suggestions, it will develop more and more within them, and it will become an unfailing source of revelation.[8]

President Joseph F. Smith declared,

> We should live so near to the Lord, be so humble in our spirits, so tractable and pliable, under the influence of the Holy Spirit, that we will be able to know the mind and the will of the Father concerning us as individuals and as officers in the Church of Christ under all circumstances. And when we live so that we can hear and understand the whisperings of the still small voice of the Spirit of God, let us do whatsoever that Spirit directs, without fear of the consequences.[9]

Peace distills into our souls as we listen to, feel, and act on the sweet promptings of the Holy Ghost.

Perfect Stillness

Just as we have to find the time and place to be still so that we can hear the voice of the Lord through the Holy Ghost, so we can be blessed with a sense of perfect stillness from the Holy Ghost.

When we are in tune with the Spirit of the Lord, and when our lives conform to what we know to be true, the stillness of peace can be ours. There is a reason why the Holy Ghost is referred to as the "still, small voice." The voice of the Holy Spirit is still and evokes stillness.

When Jezebel was seeking the life of Elijah—who then became fearful and despondent—the Lord sent an angel to comfort him, and then he was led to Mt. Horeb. There, he had a most remarkable experience. We read, "And, behold, the Lord passed by, and a great strong wind rent the mountains, and brake in pieces the rocks before the Lord; but the Lord was not in the wind: and after the wind an earthquake;

but the Lord was not in the earthquake: And after the earthquake a fire; but the Lord was not in the fire: and after the fire a still small voice" (1 Kings 19:11–12).

And so it was that with the "still, small voice" Elijah was able to hear and converse with the Lord.

We find the Lord in the "still, small voice," but we also have to be still if we are to hear Him and feel of His presence. The Psalmist counseled, "Be still, and know that I am God" (Psalm 46:10).

The Book of Mormon records that when Lehi and Nephi (the sons of Helaman) were under threat for their lives, a cloud of darkness covered the land, and the Lord's voice was heard calling the people to repentance: "It was not a voice of thunder, neither was it a voice of great tumultuous noise, but behold, it was a still voice of perfect mildness, as if it had been a whisper, and it did pierce even to the very soul" (Helaman 5:30).

When I was a bishop for the first time, a good, young adult man who was meeting with the missionaries and moving along toward baptism attended one of our testimony meetings. Although he was not a member of the Church, he rose and came forward to share his thoughts. He told us that while he was praying to find out if he should become a member of the Church, thunder, lightning, and storm suddenly filled the sky outside of his window; he had a feeling of fear and darkness, and he therefore knew that the Church could not be true. I stood up at the pulpit and testified that the Holy Ghost does not speak in thunder, lighting, and storm, nor does He instill fear or darkness. Those feelings, as at the time of Joseph Smith's first vision, did not come from heaven, and should not be heeded. I spoke then, and afterward, to him about the operation of the Holy Ghost as a "still, small voice," which leaves one with a feeling of hope, goodness, and peace.

Sadly it was to no avail, and he lost the fulness of the gospel and all that it means. It was an individual victory for Satan who was, of course, in the thunder, lightning, and storm, and who had brought a sense of fear and darkness. I have since thought that this young man would probably have gone on to be a great leader in the Church had he not allowed himself to be deceived by the father of lies.

One of the first hymns I learned as a young boy was "The Lord Is My Shepherd," based on Psalm 23. The words of that psalm and the hymn have always brought to me a sense of peace. In the King James

Version of the Bible, there is a wonderful line, "He leadeth me beside still waters" (Psalm 23:2).

The word "still" has sometimes been translated as "quiet." Although it is only one word, and could simply be glossed over, there is a world of difference between "quiet" and "still." Quietness means lack of noise; stillness means lack of motion.

During my service in the Pacific Area Presidency, Dianne and I spent an hour or two enjoying a short cruise around Milford Sound, a spectacularly scenic part of the Fjordlands in the South Island of New Zealand. It was almost breathtakingly beautiful. At a point on the cruise the captain shut down the engines, the boat came to a complete stop, and we were asked to remain noiseless. The water was still, sound ceased; we had perfect stillness, total peace. I thought of what the Savior does for us. Like the captain on the boat, the promise is this, "He leadeth me beside the still waters."

Furthermore,

> He restoreth my soul: he leadeth me in the paths of righteousness for his name's sake.
>
> Yea, though I walk through the valley of the shadow of death, I will fear no evil: for thou art with me; thy rod and thy staff they comfort me.
>
> Thou preparest a table before me in the presence of mine enemies: thou anointest my head with oil; my cup runneth over.
>
> Surely goodness and mercy shall follow me all the days of my life: and I will dwell in the house of the Lord for ever. (Psalm 23:3–6)

Through the Holy Ghost we can find ourselves beside "still" waters where there is no ripple or disturbance, just perfect stillness. We each need these moments in our lives; they bring a total endowment of love, stillness, and perfect peace through the Holy Ghost.

Perhaps the most significant place where members of the Church can feel that they are "beside still waters" is within the walls of a holy temple, "The House of the Lord." Many, myself included, can attest that when in total reverence, one sitting in the celestial room of any temple can feel a total separation from the busy cares of the world. We experience sublime serenity and the Spirit of the Lord is there.

The Holy Ghost can and does instill within us a sense of perfect stillness if we live so as to merit that all encompassing gift, and if we have tuned our spiritual radars to "receive" mode.

CHAPTER 2

Peace in the World

*I*s world peace too much to hope for?

We know that it will finally be so during the millennial reign of the Savior. We look forward to the time when, as Isaiah prophesied, "He shall judge among the nations, and shall rebuke many people: and they shall beat their swords to plowshares, and their spears into pruninghooks: nations shall not lift up sword against nation, neither shall they learn war any more" (Isaiah 2:4). Such will be the conditions when the Savior returns, when the Prince of Peace comes as King of Kings and Lord of Lords.

What a glorious prospect! Hasten the day!

Evidences of Peace

Meanwhile, can peace be obtained anywhere, or are we destined to live in the age of "wars and rumors of wars" (Matthew 24:6) spoken of by the Savior? Certainly, there have been many wars over the centuries, long years when war has seemed endemic. The first half of the twentieth century saw global conflict in two terrible wars. However, since 1945 the nations of the earth have avoided global conflict. This is a major achievement. After the breakup of the Soviet Union, Europe faced regional conflicts and ethnic cleansing in the states of the previous Yugoslavia. Power shifts and border disputes that had, in effect, been put in the freezer, thawed out and became alive again. Yet major European nations have not descended into conflict. We have demonstrated that peace is possible between nations.

Sadly, there have been, and still are, regional conflicts that have ravaged people and caused distress and destruction. Many countries in Africa have fallen foul of despots and tyrants who have been gluttonous for power, dominance, wealth, and status, more anxious about themselves than the peoples they are supposed to serve. These conflicts have been, and still are, truly awful. Luckily, for decades the major world powers have avoided being drawn into global war. Regional conflicts have largely been confined to the countries involved, even though multi-national forces at times have been engaged in bringing tyranny to an end. Thankfully, at the time I am writing, some of these hostilities appear close to resolution. Of course, acts of terrorism by extremist groups continue to plague many nations, and have yet to be eradicated.

The Book of Mormon not only records numerous wars, it also contains accounts of periods of peace. The Anti-Nephi-Lehis or Ammonites, for example, buried their swords in the ground as they made a covenant to avoid war. We read, "Now there was not one soul among all the people who had been converted unto the Lord that would take up arms against their brethren; nay, they would not even make any preparations for war; yea, and also their king commanded them that they should not" (Alma 24:6). Although peace did not endure, hostilities ended at least for a season.

Later, there was to be two hundred years of peace as recorded in 4 Nephi. Not only was this a peace between the Nephite and Lamanite nations, it was also a peace within each nation. We read, "There were no contentions and disputations among them and every man did deal justly one with another" (4 Nephi 1:2).

There came a time when national differences were forgotten, when there was no "manner of -ites; but they were in one, the children of Christ, and heirs to the kingdom of God" (4 Nephi 1:17).

So it was that "there was no contention among all the people, in all the land: but there were mighty miracles wrought among the disciples of Jesus Christ" (4 Nephi 1:13). This was an extensive condition: "There were no envyings, nor strifes, nor tumults, nor whoredoms, nor lyings, nor murders, nor any manner of lasciviousness and surely there could not be a happier people among all the people who had been created by the hand of God" (4 Nephi 1:16).

What made the difference to these war-like people? The answer is given: "The people were all converted unto the Lord" (4 Nephi 1:2) and "because of the love of God which did dwell in the hearts of the people" (4 Nephi 1:15).

If there is to be peace in our world, in our time, on this side of the Millennium, it will come not as the result of world councils, as helpful as they may be, but rather as the result of people being converted to the Lord.

An Impossible Dream?

From *Man of La Mancha* came the song "The Impossible Dream." [10] The import of the song is identifiable in the first few lines:

> To dream the impossible dream
> To fight the unbeatable foe
> To bear with unbearable sorrow
> To run where the brave dare not go
> To right the unrightable wrong
> To love pure and chaste from afar
> To try when your arms are too weary
> To reach the unreachable star
>
> This is my quest
> To follow that star
> No matter how hopeless
> No matter how far
>
> To fight for the right
> Without question or pause
> To be willing to march into Hell
> For a Heavenly cause

Is chance for peace an impossible dream? I think of the changes I have seen in my own lifetime. For decades, the end of the Cold War and freedom of nations seemed like a far off, impossible dream. Then, in his first major address as the Lord's prophet, President Spencer W. Kimball reminded the Church of the Old Testament accounts where we find the words, "Is any thing too hard for the Lord?" (Genesis 18:14). He cited the example of a child being born to Abraham and Sarah despite the fact that he was one hundred years old and she ninety with a barren womb, way past the age of reproduction. Yet they did have a son, and

15

Abraham became the father of nations. President Kimball continued, "If he commands, certainly He can fulfill. We remember the exodus of the Children of Israel crossing the uncrossable Red Sea. We remember Cyrus diverting a river and taking the impregnable city of Babylon. We remember the Lehites getting to the promised land. . . . I believe the Lord can do anything He sets His mind to do."[11]

President Kimball called on members of the Church to be prepared to enter the nations then closed to the Church. He urged us to expand our vision, and lengthen our stride. The Lord would not open doors that we were not prepared to enter. He reminded the Twelve that the Lord had said to them, as He had to Thomas B. Marsh, "I have chosen [you] to hold the keys of my kingdom . . . abroad among all nations—that thou mayest be my servant to unlock the door of the kingdom in all places" (Doctrine & Covenants 112:16–17) and "Wherefore, withersoever they shall send you, go ye, and I will be with you; and in whatsoever place ye shall proclaim my name an effectual door shall be opened unto you" (Doctrine & Covenants 112:19).

In stunning prophetic vision, President Kimball spoke of a future when the gospel would be taken to the Communist blocs of the world, "I can see no good reason why the Lord would open doors that we are not prepared to enter. Why should He break down the Iron Curtain or the Bamboo curtain . . . if we are still unprepared to enter?"[12] This was totally electrifying. Once I heard it, I knew we had heard the voice of the Lord. I knew that the vision would be fulfilled—and I had total trust in that, but I have to say that I was not sure if I would see it in my lifetime. When President Kimball gave this address we had 17,564 missionaries in the field. He called for more, many more. The following year, over 14,000 missionaries were called, a similar number in the year to follow. From 1986, the number grew to over 20,000 per year, and to over 25,000 in 1989 and 1990.

The Church responded and the Lord fulfilled the promise. The Cold War, which started at the Yalta Conference of February 1945, began to draw to an end. With the ascendency to power of Ronald Reagan in the USA, Mikhail Gorbachev in the USSR, and Margaret Thatcher in the UK, the world began to change. Pope John Paul II also played a major, if unheralded, role in supporting the pro-democracy "Solidarity" movement in Poland, which then became the first Eastern European country to become independent in June of 1989. Then the dominoes began to fall one-by-one. The Berlin Wall, long a symbol of repression, fell in November 1989. It was brought down not by men in tanks armed with missiles, but by young people in blue jeans armed with hope, sledgehammers, and pick-axes. My wife and I have stood where the wall used to be.

By the end of 1989, Communist governments fell in Czechoslovakia, Bulgaria, and Romania, and, in effect, the Soviet Empire ended. Lithuania became independent in March 1990, Germany was reunited in August of that year, and the end of the Soviet Union and the Cold War came in August of the following year.

Impossible dream? In my lifetime, it became a reality. As a result, we have missionaries in each of those former Communist controlled nations, and missionaries from those nations are now serving throughout the world. Along the way, following the specific apostolic work of President Thomas S. Monson, the Freiberg Germany Temple, announced in 1982, was dedicated in June 1985, five years before the unification of Germany.

As Elder George Q. Cannon taught, "Every foundation that is laid for a temple, and every temple completed . . . lessens the power of Satan in the earth."[13]

It is little wonder that the construction of a temple in what was East Germany preceded the breakup of the Soviet Empire. We now have a temple in Ukraine, and no doubt more will follow in these previously Communist countries. It is a changed world. We live in an era of miracles, when impossible dreams come to pass.

We are yet to see the fulfillment of the second half of President Kimball's prophecy. The Bamboo Curtain is still intact.

Role of the Restoration

We often hear words to the effect that, if there is a God why does He not do something about the state of the world? Why does He not stop it all? It is the message, mission, and witness of The Church of Jesus Christ of Latter-day Saints that there is a God, and He *has* done something. As we read in the preface to the Doctrine & Covenants:

> Wherefore, I the Lord, knowing the calamity which should come upon the inhabitants of the earth, called upon my servant Joseph Smith Jun., and spake unto him from heaven, and gave him

commandments; And also gave commandments to others, that they should proclaim these things unto the world, and all this that it might be fulfilled, which was written by the prophets—The weak things of the world shall come forth and break down the mighty and strong ones, that man should not counsel his fellow man, neither trust in the arm of flesh . . . that faith might also increase in the earth. (Doctrine & Covenants 1:17–21)

This is the clarion message of the Church. Simply put, it is that there is a God; He is not dead; He does not sleep. He knows of the calamity of the world and has prepared a cure from before the foundations of the world that is central to His plan for the happiness of all of His children. This cure is found in the teachings, commandments, and ordinances of the gospel of Jesus Christ in their fulness.

While many may pray and hope for "world peace" it is the spread of the gospel through the work of the "messengers of peace," the missionaries of the Church, that the promise will be fulfilled. It was when the Church had enough missionaries, as President Kimball had called for, that the miracles occurred. It will continue, nation upon nation, as the gospel is preached and accepted. As Isaiah prophesied, "How beautiful upon the mountains are the feet of him that . . . publisheth salvation; that saith unto Zion, Thy God reigneth" (Isaiah 52:7).

The missionaries of the Church are the messengers of peace. Wherever the Church is established, we do good and the nation is blessed.

In 1949, the First Presidency of the Church stated, "Only through a return to the teachings of the Master can peace come to the world, and the kingdom of God can be made ready for the return of the Prince of Peace, to reign as King of Kings, and Lord of Lords."[14]

If the teachings of the Master are to have that effect, they have to be taken to all the world. That is why the Savior in His final direction to the early apostles delivered the imperative to go "into all the world, and preach the gospel to every creature. He that believeth and is baptized shall be saved" (Mark 16:15–16).

Such a work may seem to stretch into perpetuity, but remember, "Is anything too hard for the Lord?" The answer is "no." As noted earlier, President Spencer W. Kimball spoke of the need for members of the Church to rise up in preparation so that the Lord could then "open the doors." The Church did and Communist regimes began to topple like dominoes.

A change in the world, through conversion, can be realized. As penned by lyricist Vince Gill, "Let there be peace on earth / and let it begin with me."[15] There is great truth in these sentiments; a striving for peace has to start with each of us, without our assuming that the responsibility rests with others.

In what may be considered a second British National Anthem, "I Vow to Thee, My Country," come words that make a powerful connection between world peace and the ways of Christ. The first verse speaks of loyalty to country, "I vow to thee, my country, all earthly things above, / Entire and whole and perfect, the service of my love;"

The third verse refers to "another country, I've heard of long ago," and concludes with the words, "And her ways are ways of gentleness, and all her paths are peace."[16] The sentiments here are that our allegiance to, and service on behalf of, our own country is noble and good, and yet of even greater significance is our allegiance to the cause of expanding the reach—the borders—of the kingdom of God on earth. It is in this latter endeavor that find us in the "ways of gentleness," and "the paths of peace." This is a work, a service, in which we can be engaged by seeking in love and faith to bring others to Christ.

President Ezra Taft Benson said, "The Lord works from the inside out. The world works from the outside in. The world would take people out of the slums. Christ takes the slums out of people, and then they take themselves out of the slums. The world would mold men by changing their environment. Christ changes men, who then change their environment. The world would shape human behavior, but Christ can change human nature."[17]

President David O. McKay wrote,

> Peace is not found in selfishness, but in striving to help make the world better and happier.
>
> I know of no better way to bring about harmony in the home, in the neighborhood, in organizations, peace in our country, and in the world than for every man and woman first to eliminate from his or her own heart, the enemies of harmony and peace such as hatred, selfishness, greed, animosity, and envy.[18]

Of course, it is often said that there have been more wars fought for religion than for any other reason. Although this may suit the agendas of secular men, the prejudiced, and the cult of atheism, it is not true; it is a fallacy. The invocation of "religion" has been the euphemism, or convenient label, that has been attached to ethnic or nationalistic war stemming from the desires of land-grabbers,: by those who are power hungry and evil. "In their *Encyclopedia of Wars*, authors Charles Phillips and Alex Axelrod attempt a comprehensive listing of wars in history. They document 1763 wars overall, of which 123 (7 percent) have been classified to involve a religious conflict."[19]

The fact is that true religion, the fulness of the gospel of Jesus Christ, is the only way to end all war.

Announcing the Savior's birth to the shepherds, the angels sang a song of peace. The King James Version of the Bible translates their message as, "Glory to God in the highest, and on earth peace, goodwill toward men" (Luke 2:14).

Frederic Farrar proposed an alternative translation: "peace among men of good will," or "peace among men with whom He is well pleased."[20]

An increase of men and women with whom God is pleased will herald peace.

In December 1949, the First Presidency of the Church stated, "Before peace can reign, there must be manifest in human hearts more compassion and less hatred; more generosity, and less greed; more sanctity in the home, fewer divorces; more guardianship, less neglect of children; more temperance, less drunkenness, more chastity, less debauchery—in a word, there must be more seeking first "the kingdom of God and His righteousness."[21]

This is not merely a trite platitude; it is the restatement of an eternal truth, which men must sooner or later accept if they would prevent the human race from further degeneration. The time has come when men's hearts must be changed, impossible though this seems to many. Man must be "born again" said Jesus Christ, whose mission on earth was to give light to them that sit in darkness and in the shadow of death, to guide our feet in the way of peace. In other words, it is through personal conversion to the gospel of Jesus Christ and the subsequent obedience to His commandments that will bring about the changes necessary to deliver widespread peace.

Of course, scripture suggests that immediately prior to the commencement of the Millenium, there will be a final global conflict centered in Israel—a conflict referred to as "Armageddon."

In Zechariah we read that "all nations [will come] against Jerusalem to battle" (Zechariah 14:2), with the result that "there shall be a great mourning in Jerusalem . . . in the valley of Megiddon. And the land shall mourn" (Zechariah 12:11, 12). "Then shall the Lord go forth and fight against those nations" (Zechariah 14:3). He said, "in that day I will seek to destroy all the nations that come against Jerusalem (Zechariah 12:9).

John the Revelator also saw this conflict in his great vision, specifically referring to the place of "Armageddon" (see Revelation 16:14–21). Elder Bruce R. McConkie, a former member of the Quorum of the Twelve Apostles, commented that this war, covering at least the entire area from Jerusalem to Meggido, will be in progress, at "the very moment of the Second Coming of our Lord."[22]

Does this mean that our efforts are futile? Surely we can prepare the world not for war, but for peace. At the end of that final war, there will have to be men and women ready to begin the work of the Lord's kingdom on earth. So there is purpose and hope in striving for peace in the world soul-by-soul.

It could be said that today's moral decay, when men "call evil good, and good evil" (Isaiah 5:20), is its own Armageddon, making it even more imperative to spread the gospel of peace.

President David O. McKay said, "Peace as taught by the Savior is exemption from individual troubles, from family broils, from irrational difficulties. Such peace refers to the person just as much as it does to communities . . . peace does not come to the transgressor of law, peace comes by obedience to the law."[23]

President Joseph F. Smith wrote, "There is only one thing that can bring peace into the world. It is the adoption of the gospel of Jesus Christ, rightly understood, obeyed, and practiced by rulers and people alike."[24]

Is world peace too much to hope for? No, it is what we are working for. We can "dream the impossible dream," and then work to make it a reality. There is nothing that is "too hard for the Lord."

CHAPTER 3

Peace through Forgiveness

A soul that is troubled by unrepented transgression can never be at peace. No matter how much good is done by that individual, unresolved sin will always prevent the receipt of total peace.

I have written elsewhere about the need for and the steps of complete repentance.[25] Suffice it here to review how true, full, and complete repentance brings peace.

Elder Francis M. Lyman taught, "The forgiveness of sins is predicated upon faith in God, repentance and reformation . . . if a man would have his sins forgiven . . . he must have faith in God, and in His Son Jesus Christ and in the Holy Ghost, he must repent of all his sins, turn unto the Lord with full purpose of heart and sin no more. Then God will forgive him and redeem him from his sins."[26]

The feelings of forgiveness and redemption will come via the Holy Ghost who will fill us with joy when full repentance is complete. President Marion G. Romney said, "Receiving the Holy Ghost is the therapy [that affects] forgiveness and heals the sin-sick soul."[27]

President Spencer W. Kimball in his seminal work *The Miracle of Forgiveness* taught, "The essence of the miracle of forgiveness is that it brings peace to the previously anxious, restless, frustrated, perhaps tormented soul."[28]

Repentance is fundamental to the receipt of feelings of peace. If the Holy Ghost is to whisper peace to our souls, we must have "cleaned house" first.

In addition, there is another type of forgiveness that is necessary if we are to completely feel a deep sense of peace: it is how ready we are to forgive others. If we are not at peace with our neighbors, it is terribly hard to be at peace with ourselves. Feelings of angst, bitterness, hatred, malice, rivalry, and vengeance are guaranteed to destroy any sense of personal peace.

As the Apostle John wrote, "If a man say, I love God, and hateth his brother, he is a liar: for he that loveth not his brother whom he hath seen, how can he love God whom he hath not seen?" (1 John 4:20). A good question. Of course, the answer is he cannot; and if he is a liar and cannot love God or his brother, then he will be troubled in heart, mind, and soul. Such a man or woman will not be at peace; it would be impossible.

It is extremely sad to see someone who is totally obsessed with feelings of malice and anger against those they feel have done them wrong. Such feelings are like a worm in an apple, or a bad apple in a barrel. It gnaws away at the soul until all feelings are soured. The person who harbors such animosity toward another is never at peace, he or she becomes twisted and bitter inside and out. No matter what the other party does, it is never enough. It is not only every fault that is magnified out of all proportion, the other party's every action is treated with disdain and contempt.

Interestingly, such malice usually has no effect whatsoever on those to whom it is targeted: they move right along making progress in life, often blissfully unaware of the rotting hate that is eating away within those who feel they have been wronged. The twisted malice really only has deleterious effect on the one who harbors the feelings. It is tragic really. I have personally seen what happens to those who harbor grudges; it is truly awful as they lose all sense of reason, they lose their way, and often lose other things that are truly important and good in their lives. Bitterness never brings bliss, but forgiveness forges fulfillment and friendship.

President Spencer W. Kimball wrote,

> It is extremely hurtful for any man [or woman] holding the gift of the Holy Ghost to harbor a spirit of envy, or malice, or retaliation, or intolerance toward or against his fellowman. We ought to say in our hearts, "Let God judge between me and thee but as for me, I will forgive . . ." I want to say to you that Latter-day Saints who harbor a feeling of unforgiveness in their souls are more censurable than the

one who has sinned against them. Go home and dismiss envy and hatred from your hearts: dismiss the feeling of unforgiveness; and cultivate in your souls that spirit of Christ which cried out upon the cross, "Father, forgive them; for they know not what they do." This is the spirit that Latter-day saints ought to possess all the day long.[29]

President Kimball also quoted President Joseph F. Smith, who in 1902 said, "We hope and pray that you will . . . forgive one another and never from this time forth . . . bear malice toward another fellow creature."[30]

There can often also be the rather miserable view of the offended that the offender must make some supernal act of contrition before there can ever be any thought of forgiveness. In this regard, President Spencer W. Kimball taught, "A common error is the idea that the offender must apologize and humble himself to the dust before forgiveness is required . . . as for the offended one, he must forgive the offender regardless of the attitude of the other. Sometimes men get satisfaction from seeing the other party on his knees and groveling in the dust, but that is not the gospel way."[31]

As we contemplate our capacity to forgive others, it is well to consider this question: "If the forgiveness I hope to receive from the Lord is commensurate with the forgiveness I extend to others, would I be happy?"

The Savior taught a powerful parable in this regard as recorded in the Gospel of Luke in which a man sought forgiveness of his debt owed to the king, at the same time as throwing into prison one who could not pay a debt to him. When word of what had happened reached the king, his reaction was justifiably furious:

"O thou wicked servant, I forgave thee all that debt, because thou desiredst me: Shouldest not thou also have had compassion on thy fellowservant, even as I had pity on thee?" (Matthew 18:32–33).

The Savior concluded His parable with the affirmation, "So likewise shall my Heavenly Father do also unto you, if ye from your hearts forgive not every one his brother their trespasses" (Matthew 18:35).

President N. Eldon Tanner put it this way: "How wonderful it would be if we would all forgive and love our neighbors. Then it would be much easier for us to call upon the Lord to forgive us of any of our wrongdoings, and as we repent and bring forth fruits meet for repentance, we can expect God's forgiveness and mercy to be extended in our behalf."[32]

In this regard, two examples are illustrative. The first is from the early days of the Church. The wife of Thomas B. Marsh, then president of the Quorum of the Twelve, fell out with another sister over something as trivial as cream. A dispute followed in which Sister Marsh was clearly the one at fault. However, when the cause was not supported by a series of Church councils—home teachers, the bishopric, the high council, and ultimately the First Presidency—both she and her husband became bitter and resentful toward the Church and left it, Brother Marsh at the cost of his position in the Quorum of the Twelve Apostles. As if that was not bad enough, his pursuit of the matter through the civil courts was a factor that led to the extermination order issued by Governor Boggs which resulted in the expulsion of fifteen thousand saints from Missouri.

Nineteen years later, Brother Marsh sought rapprochement with the Church. Making his way to Salt Lake City, he asked President Brigham Young for forgiveness. Later, he wrote, "The Lord could get along very well without me and He . . . lost nothing by my falling out of the ranks; but O what have I lost?! Riches, greater riches than all this world or many planets like this could afford."[33]

In stark, and almost overwhelmingly inspiring, contrast we have the more recent example of the reaction of the Amish people in Pennsylvania following the murder of five girls and injury of another five by a crazed milkman neighbor who suddenly and inexplicably ran amok in October 2006 before killing himself.

The reaction of the Amish people was nothing short of extraordinary. They forgave immediately, and as one began to reach out to the perpetrator's family in love and support. One wrapped his arms around the dead man's father and said, "We will forgive you." Half of the mourners at the gunman's funeral were Amish, and when money was received from well-wishers to pay for the health care of the injured girls and the burial expenses of the other five, the Amish shared it with the widow of the gunman and their three children. The family of the murderer issued this public statement,

> Our family wants each of you to know that we are overwhelmed by the forgiveness, grace, and mercy that you've extended to us. Your love for our family has helped to provide the healing we so desperately need. The prayers, flowers, cards and gifts you've given have touched our hearts in a way no words can describe. Your compassion

has reached beyond our family, beyond our community, and is changing our world, and for this we sincerely thank you.[34]

The penetrating question for each of us as we contemplate our reaction to those we feel have wronged us is, "Will I be a Thomas Marsh, or one of the Amish?" Might our eternal lives depend on the answer?

A related matter is how we regard those around us in general. Many personal and institutional relationships are soured by an indulgence in judging others. We hear of the angst and trouble caused by the ostracizing of those whose lifestyles are perhaps not in keeping with what might be considered the "norm" or the "expected," or of others being treated badly because they do not share a common faith. One wonders why some feel that they have been given a kind of divine right to judge and interfere with others. Our communities would be happier if each kept their noses out of other people's business. The Savior only intervenes in our lives if we invite Him to do so. It is an example we would do well to follow.

There is such individual peace that we can feel if we repent of our own sins and make allowances for the deeds of others, even if we think they are in the wrong.

Our ability to obtain peace through forgiveness, for ourselves and those with whom we interact is enhanced when we cultivate lives of peace and goodness, which always "spill over" into our treatment of others. We can then, with certain confidence, call upon the Lord to forgive our transgressions and obtain peace in every aspect of our lives. It starts in our own homes.

Of course, all of our ways should be ways of peace. In our homes we should each be the bringer of peace, and a peacemaker when that is required. One of the qualities that I admire most in our youngest son is his ever-present capacity to bring peace to every situation. Whenever tension of any kind has arisen in our home, the spell has often been broken by one of his cheering remarks or insightful comments.

Elder George Q. Cannon taught, "Husbands when they go into their homes ought to carry with them a spirit of peace and joy, so that all might be cheered by his presence, the children glad to meet him, glad to have him come, and sorry when he goes away and the wife, on her part, gladdened by the same spirit."[35]

The same should be true of every family member. In a powerful teaching, President J. Reuben Clark said,

Each Christian is armed with a sword by which he is to divide the old law from the new covenant, the ritual of sacrifice for the simple righteousness of life; by which he cleaves from his soul all that is base and ignoble in him, and these being destroyed and cast out of his life, then comes the blessed peace from him who promised peace—not the peace of the world of ease, luxury, idleness, absence of turmoil and strife, but the peace born of the righteous life: the peace that lifts the soul: the peace that, day by day, brings us ever nearer to the home of Eternal Peace, the dwelling place of our Father. [36]

Achieving such abiding peace depends on lack of pride and is a daily endeavor. Elder George Q. Cannon said:

This meek, humble, broken, and contrite spirit . . . will produce union and love. . . . It is the duty of every man and woman in this Church to live at peace with him and herself, and then to live at peace with everybody else, husbands with wives, wives with husbands, parents with children, children with parents, brothers with sisters and sisters with brothers; this is the duty that God requires at our hands. I am speaking now of something which is not abstract theory, that cannot be carried out; I am speaking of that which can be carried out, which every one of us can carry out, and of results which can be accomplished in the midst of this people.[37]

I doubt that any one of us is perfect in this regard, but I know that inner peace, the peace of the soul, the peace "which passeth all understanding" (Philippians 4:7), can dwell with each of us. It is attainable.

President John Taylor quoted the Savior's precious words, "My peace I give unto you: not as the world giveth, give I unto you" (John 14:27), before teaching, "Wherever this peace exists, it leaves an influence that is comforting and refreshing to the souls of those who partake of it. It is like the morning dew to the thirsty plant. This peace is alone the gift of God, and it can only be received from Him through obedience to His laws."[38]

Isaiah proclaimed, "How beautiful upon the mountains are the feet of him that bringeth good tidings, that publisheth peace; that bringeth good tidings of good, that publisheth salvation" (Isaiah 52:7).

As mentioned earlier, I have always associated this verse with the work of our full-time missionaries. They did, after all, bring the message of peace to my mother and henceforth into my life, as they do day by day, country by country, and family by family.

I witnessed an exquisite example of how such peace can come through the humble actions of one of the Lord's missionaries in Tarawa on the islands of Kiribati. I was there on assignment and while a small group of us—the missionaries, the wife of the mission president, and I—were waiting, the mission president's wife suddenly noticed that one of our missionaries from Papua New Guinea had shoes that were literally falling apart. It was not possible to obtain shoes on the islands, so the president and his wife were in the habit of taking a tracing of the feet of a missionary and using it to purchase shoes when they were passing through Honolulu on their way back to the mission home in Majuro, Marshall Islands.

Seeing the state of the shoes of this sweet young missionary, the mission president's wife said, "We need to take a tracing of your feet." Immediately, one of the other missionaries obtained paper and a pencil and knelt down at the feet of the young missionary. Now this young man who knelt down looked like the All-American boy of substance: tall, good looking, and confident. I could envision him in a fairly prosperous home, on the sports field, behind the steering wheel of a classy car, attending an Ivy League school in a blazer, tie, and dress pants.

Now, here he was, without hesitation, kneeling at the feet of another man who came from a country where most people still live in makeshift homes in jungle clearings, without electricity, sanitation, or running water. The American missionary removed the other's shoes, and then carefully peeled his socks off. He then said, "You have beautiful feet." Now the toes of the other missionary were splayed in all kinds of directions, as is common on a Pacific Islander who has never worn shoes.

As I observed this act of selfless love, I obtained a whole new perspective on the scripture, "How beautiful . . . are the feet" (Isaiah 52:7). I felt very touched and humbled, and a feeling of unparalleled peace filled that little room.

The conclusion of this chapter is best set out by President John Taylor, "If any man wishes to introduce peace into his family or among his friends, let him cultivate it in his own bosom; for sterling peace can only be had according to the legitimate rule and authority of heaven, and obedience to its laws."[39]

Perhaps one of the most significant ways in which this "sterling peace" can be realized, in our own lives and in the lives of others, comes when we obtain forgiveness for ourselves and extend it to others. The spread of the gospel, and the love that originates with Jesus Christ, can and does instill peace and harmony if we allow it to do so.

The gospel alters our thinking, and as illustrated by the missionary in Tarawa, we begin to focus on love and service rather than revenge or guilt and introspection.

There is peace in forgiveness.

CHAPTER 4

Peace amidst Adversity

*T*here will come a time when we can leave adversity behind and, with the Lord's help, emerge from darkness into an abundance of light.

Peace can be restored. Troubled turmoil can give way to mollifying mildness.

Interestingly, the Apostle Paul used the analogy of light in explaining how he could testify that "we are troubled on every side, yet not distressed; we are perplexed, but not in despair; Persecuted, but not forsaken; cast down, but not destroyed" (2 Corinthians 4:8–9).

Paul sets out how he was able to rise above the persecution and rejection: "For God, who commanded the light to shine out of darkness, hath shined in our hearts, to give the light of the knowledge of the glory of God in the face of Jesus Christ" (2 Corinthians 4:6).

Most of us at some time in our lives feel the chilled winds of adversity. Storms brew, rains fall, winds blow, and floods rise. It may seem that there is no end in sight, that we simply face a future of uncertainty and doubt, trial and tribulation.

We should not be surprised when we find ourselves in the midst of adversity. It is meant to be that way. Elder Joseph B. Wirthlin taught

> Life was made for struggle; and exaltation, success, and victory were never meant to be cheap or to come easily. The tides of life often challenge us. To understand why it has to be this way, we should maintain our understanding, our faith, and our courage by a constant rereading of Second Nephi, chapter two, the substance of which is

set forth in this excerpt: "For it must needs be there is an opposition in all things" (2 Nephi 2:11).

Now let me make a suggestion that will enable us to maintain our spiritual strength and keep our testimonies vitally alive so that the trials, the storms, and the tides of life will not defeat us. This suggestion is that, above all, we should heed the words of Jesus to the woman at Jacob's well in Samaria when he said, "Whosoever drinketh of the water that I shall give him will never thirst; but the water that I shall give him shall be in him a well of water springing up into everlasting life" (John 4:14).

How could one's strength ebb or falter when it may be so dependably and continuously nourished and restored? Here it is made clear that life, at its best and most vigorous, is spiritual and, as such, is the sincere expression of the soul to God. The spiritual self of each of us is that part of us that will never grow old, or ill, or die, but it must be nurtured and invigorated! Drinking of the living water is the unique recipe, the only way![40]

Many are familiar with the oft quoted poem "Good Timber" by Douglas Malloch. The third stanza reads:

Good timber does not grow in ease,
The stronger the wind, the stronger trees
The farther sky, the greater length
The more the storm, the more the strength.
By sun and cold, by rain and snow,
In tree and men good timbers grow.[41]

As well as experiencing periodic thunderstorms, we can experience horrific hurricanes and tempests of turmoil that can destroy our confidence, disturb our peace, and shake our sense of self-worth. All that we hold dear can suddenly feel so ephemeral, like it is slipping through our fingers. Major life changes can knock us off balance, disrupting our sense of equilibrium.

Perhaps an unexpected layoff has led to long-term unemployment, lack of financial freedom has cut choice, or mortgage meltdown has left us in monetary misery. Perhaps anticipated retirement after a long, busy, and productive career has brought a sense of loss. Perhaps sudden sickness or devastating disability has left us feeling boxed in, helpless, hopeless, and uncertain. In such circumstances, fear can come easily, while faith can be hard to sustain.

All of this is normal. President Boyd K. Packer has taught that there is purpose in our struggles in life:

> We are indoctrinated that somehow we should always be instantly emotionally comfortable, when that is not so, some become anxious—and all too frequently seek relief from counseling, from analysis, and even from medication.
>
> It was meant to be that life would be a challenge. To suffer some anxiety, some depression, some disappointment, even some failure is normal.
>
> Teach our members that if they have a good, miserable day once in a while, or several in a row, to stand steady and face them. Things will straighten out.
>
> There is great purpose in our struggle in life.[42]

I know all of this for myself. While recovering from surgery to remove two sizeable brain tumors, I experienced periods of melancholy and dismay from the emotional and mental impact of it all. I discovered that I was not as invincible as I once thought I was. Medication did not help and a relapse or two brought additional despondency. I began to feel sorry for myself. I cried to heaven for relief, and it came. I had an experience akin to that recorded by Helaman in an account of a great war, about 74 BC, between the Nephites and the Lamanites, with Moroni as the leader of the Nephites. The Lamanites, under the avaricious aspirations of Amalikiah, had become even more ferocious and voracious in their thirst for possessions, land, and power. Sadly, they were joined by some dissenting Nephites. In the midst of it all, Helaman, the son of Alma, sought to defend the religious liberty of the people whilst fulfilling his father's final injunction to build up and establish the Church.

As the war drew to its conclusion, and Helaman was reflecting on its progress, he writes of the time when needed help and reinforcements had not arrived to sustain them in the midst of their calamities. "The cause why they did not send more strength unto us, we know not; therefore we were grieved and also filled with fear, lest by any means the judgments of God should come upon our land, to our overthrow and utter destruction" (Alma 58:9).

Some of us who have not received the much-needed help and support we feel we need to protect and lift us from our present conditions can likewise be filled with fear and grief. We may fear that we are at an end, that all that we hold dear may be "overthrown" and lost; in effect, that the circumstances of life are leading to our "utter destruction." Even if such feelings can, at times, seem over-dramatic, they nevertheless come to those who feel an almost overwhelming sense of loss and emotional angst.

Then Helaman records something refreshingly rejuvenating:

> Therefore, we did pour out our souls in prayer to God, that he would strengthen us and deliver us out of the hands of our enemies, yea, and give us strength that we might retain our cities, and our lands, and our possessions, for the support of our people.
>
> Yea, and it came to pass that the Lord our God did visit us with assurances that he would deliver us; yea, insomuch that *he did speak peace to our souls*, and did grant unto us great faith, and did cause us that we should hope for our deliverance in him. (Alma 58:10–11, emphasis added)

Something wonderful happened. The calamity was not instantly removed, but in response to their humility, to their recognition of their dependence on God, and to their prayers drawn from their very souls, they felt assurances from heaven that all would be well, that all would work out, and that deliverance would come. They received strength to retain what was precious. Peace was spoken to their minds and they were strengthened by greater faith and hope.

So it can be for us. Our world can turn upside down so that it may seem like we are being attacked from all sides. If one calamity is not bad enough, they can come all at once: piling on top of us, leaving at times not even a glimmer of light. Disturbance can be all around us. We feel our own deep grief; even though no one has actually died, something inside us has, or at least it is only functioning on life support. At this point some, aided by the woeful whisperings of the evil one who wants to make us as miserable as himself, can be tempted to give up, shut down, suffer emotional breakdown, even contemplate, attempt, or commit suicide. There is modern evidence of such despair now rising from European countries where economic collapse and severe austerity measures have taken their toll on the mental conditions and emotional stability of an increasing number of people.[43] In the midst of World War II, a British inspirational poster counseled "Keep calm and carry on." It is as good advice for our time as it was then.

Without trivializing any of this, the truth is that assurances that are needed will not come from banks, collection agencies, ministries, pension funds, or politicians. Blessed assurance, faith, hope, and peace comes in and through the Prince of Peace. Amongst members of the Church, the relief that is needed with hope, faith, assurance, and peace is only obtainable from heaven. It comes to us as it came to the people of Helaman: as a result of soul-stretching, humble prayer, righteous desires, and a willingness to personally do all that was necessary for relief to come.

In a landmark address entitled "The Atonement" during the October 2012 general conference, President Boyd K. Packer, President of the Quorum of the Twelve Apostles, spoke of the healing effects of the Savior's Atonement in these terms:

> If you have made no mistakes, then you do not need the Atonement. If you have made mistakes, and all of us have, whether minor or serious, then you have an enormous need to find out how they can be erased so that you are no longer in darkness. . . .
>
> No matter what our transgressions have been, no matter how much our actions may have hurt others, that guilt can all be wiped out. To me, perhaps the most beautiful phrase in all scripture is when the Lord said, "Behold, he who has repented of his sins, the same is forgiven, and I, the Lord, remember them no more."

Concluding his remarks, President Packer testified, "Wherever our members and missionaries go, our message is one of faith and hope in the Savior Jesus Christ," and he then quoted the lyrics of this hymn, "Does the Journey Seem Long," written by President Joseph Fielding Smith:

> 1. Does the journey seem long,
> The path rugged and steep?
> Are there briars and thorns on the way?
> Do sharp stones cut your feet
> As you struggle to rise
> To the heights thru the heat of the day?
>
> 2. Is your heart faint and sad,
> Your soul weary within,
> As you toil 'neath your burden of care?
> Does the load heavy seem
> You are forced now to lift?
> Is there no one your burden to share?

3. Let your heart be not faint
Now the journey's begun;
There is One who still beckons to you.
So look upward in joy
And take hold of his hand;
He will lead you to heights that are new—

4. A land holy and pure,
Where all trouble doth end,
And your life shall be free from all sin,
Where no tears shall be shed,
For no sorrows remain.
Take his hand and with him enter in.

Immediately following his inspiring talk, the Tabernacle Choir, with Shane Warby as soloist, sang the hymn. It was exquisite; a feeling of peace and consolation swept over me and tears were shed. We can indeed "look upward in joy" despite the briars and thorns in our way.[44]

As was noted earlier when the humble followers of Christ were under grief-causing attack, "Nevertheless they did fast and pray oft, and did wax stronger and stronger in their humility, and firmer and firmer in the faith of Christ, unto the filling their souls with joy and consolation, yea, even to the purifying and the sanctification of their hearts, which sanctification cometh because of their yielding their hearts unto God" (Helaman 3:35).

The message is clear. In the midst of personal tumult, stand fast; hold the course; exercise humility and faith; renew your covenant to yield yourself to God; fast and pray all-consuming, fiber-stretching, soul-wrenching prayers; and then wait for the condescension of God. Precious assurance and strength will come; peace will follow.

Decide to Be Happy

For me, in the midst of my melancholy that followed brain surgery, radiation, and chemotherapy, some wonderful things began to happen. Good friends and trusted Church leaders offered their support and understanding, and I began to listen to their counsel and accept their encouragement. Late one night as I shared my gloomy feelings with our youngest son, he said, "Well, Dad, I have always thought that happiness is a decision." He is right.

I found myself increasingly expressing gratitude for all the blessings I still enjoyed. I discovered for myself that "this kind goeth not out but by prayer and fasting" (Matthew 17:21).

I felt the strength, power, and love of the Savior. With Paul, I came to rejoice in the knowledge that tribulation, distress, and peril could not separate me from the love of Christ (see Romans 8:35).

Fortunately, the hopeful and certain truth is that, no matter what, we can find strength and encouragement. Our burdens can become lighter, even if they do not suddenly go away. We can emerge on the other side of the darkest abyss, stronger and more resolute, better men and better women.

From *The Count of Monte Cristo* by Alexandre Dumas comes a conversation between the main character, Edmund Dantes, and his fellow prisoner, Abbe Faria. The young Dantes expressed wonder at all the Abbe had accomplished while held captive, and remarked that the Abbe would have accomplished even more had he been free. The Abbe, who had been held captive for eleven years in a doleful, dismal dungeon cell, stated that perhaps he needed the oppression and difficulty to enable his accomplishments. He then said, "Captivity has collected into one single focus all the floating faculties of my mind; they have come into close contact in the narrow space in which they have been wedged. You know that from the collision of clouds electricity is produced, and from electricity comes the lightning from whose flash we have light amid our greatest darkness."[45]

In the furnace of life's afflictions, we develop God-like attributes. Elder Neal A. Maxwell wrote,

> In life, the sandpaper of circumstances often smoothes our crustiness and patiently polishes our rough edges. There is nothing pleasant about it, however. And the Lord will go to great lengths in order to teach us a particular lesson and to help us to overcome a particular weakness, especially if there is no other way. In such circumstances, it is quite useless for us mortals to try to do our own sums when it comes to suffering. We can't make it all add up because clearly we do not have all the numbers. Furthermore, none of us knows much about the algebra of affliction. The challenges that come are shaped to our needs and circumstances, sometimes in order to help our weaknesses become strengths. Job noted how tailored his challenges were, saying, "For the thing which I greatly feared has come upon me, and that which I was afraid of is come unto me" (Job 3:25). Yet

he prevailed so much so that he was held up as a model to the great latter-day prophet, Joseph Smith (Doctrine & Covenants 121). Our triumph here could not be complete if we merely carried our fears and doubts into the next world. What came to Job was not a minor test with which he could have coped with one hand tied behind him. Rather, "his grief was very great" (Job 2:13).[46]

Having been proven in the crucible of affliction, we will have cultivated a character that is able to face and withstand future life shocks. As a result, we can use our experiences to lift and empathize with others. Our own example of personal perseverance can give hope to others and inspire our families. We become more fit for the future.

Elder Orson F. Whitney said, "No pain that we suffer, no trial that we experience is wasted. It ministers to our education, to the development of such qualities as patience, faith, fortitude, and humility. All that we suffer and all that we endure, especially when we endure it patiently, builds up our characters, purifies our hearts, expands our souls, and makes us more tender and charitable, more worthy to be called the children of God."[47]

Over time we can also feel the Lord's blessings, and our circumstances can change dramatically. In the talk I delivered during the April 2012 general conference of the Church, I referred to the circumstance of a divorced mother of seven.

In the general Relief Society meeting of September 2006, President Gordon B. Hinckley related an experience shared by a divorced single mother of seven children then ranging in age from seven to sixteen. She had gone across the street to deliver something to a neighbor. She said:

> As I turned around to walk back home, I could see my house lighted up. I could hear echoes of my children as I had walked out of the door a few minutes earlier. They were saying: "'Mom, what are we going to have for dinner?" "Can you take me to the library?" "I have to get some poster paper tonight." Tired and weary, I looked at that house and saw the light on in each of the rooms. I thought of all of those children who were home waiting for me to come and meet their needs. My burdens felt heavier than I could bear.
>
> I remember looking through tears toward the sky, and I said, "Dear Father, I just can't do it tonight. I'm too tired. I can't face it. I can't go home and take care of all those children alone. Could I just come to You and stay with You for just one night? . . ."

I didn't really hear the words of reply, but I heard them in my mind. The answer was: "No, little one, you can't come to me now. . . . But I can come to you." [48]

Following general conference I learned something of the rest of the story from the new husband of that single mother. "The seven children are now grown, have served six missions, are all married in the temple, are busy with church callings, and have a total of twenty-four children. Temporally we can count in their numbers, including their spouses, a graduate of Harvard Law School, an MBA from BYU, a dentist, an army medical officer, and a significant software business success."

The narrative continued, "Even more, they are close as a family and enjoy time together immensely. The last is a special legacy of their mother who, despite challenges, retained her optimism, love, and sense of life."[49]

While adversity may be slow to leave us, *we can choose* to leave it at any time. The Lord's promise to us is as it was to Alma and his people in the midst of horrendous persecution: "And I will also ease the burdens which are put upon your shoulders, that even you cannot feel them upon your backs" (Mosiah 24:14).

Furthermore, the Lord has confirmed, "I will not leave you comfortless: I will come to you" (John 14:18).

Heavenly help may not be obvious. We may not immediately see or know that some other burdens that would have come our way have been lifted or diverted from our door.

The Lord assures, "Behold, verily, verily, I say unto you that mine eyes are upon you. I am in your midst and ye cannot see me" (Doctrine & Covenants 38:7).

Of course, we may need to be supremely patient with others and ourselves. It often takes time for everything to work out. Even if at times our faith seems no bigger than a mustard seed, as we move forward, providence will move with us. If we seek heaven's help, we will receive it—perhaps even in unexpected ways.

We can find the wherewithal to be thankful for what we have, rather than mourn what we have lost. Interestingly, we often hear that same sentiment expressed by those who have lost all of their worldly possessions in a natural disaster such as a wildfire, a flood, or a hurricane. In virtually every case they say, "At least we still have what is really important."

The testimony of Paul is encouraging: "I have learned, in whatsoever state I am, therewith to be content. I know both how to be abased, and I know how to abound: every where and in all things I am instructed both to be full and to be hungry, both to abound and to suffer need. I can do all things through Christ which strengtheneth me" (Philippians 4:11–13).

As has been written, "All that is unfair about life can be made right through the Atonement of Jesus Christ."[50]

Despite adversity, perhaps at times even because of it, we can obtain a greater sense of peace. Whatever our circumstances, there will come a time when we can leave adversity behind and, with the Lord's help, emerge from darkness into an abundance of light.

Gospel light brings deep and abiding peace.

CHAPTER 5

Peace amidst Death

*T*he passing of a loved one is, perhaps, the most significant disrupter of personal peace, made more bitter if that person has died young or has taken their own life. Of course we mourn, we feel loss, we grieve. It is sometimes said that the grief we feel will come to an end in this life. I am not so sure.

At the memorial service for those who died in the terrorist attacks on New York's Twin Towers in September 2011, the message from Queen Elizabeth II included the words, "Grief is the price we pay for love." This is a marvelous insight.

When one is deeply loved, grief can feel almost overwhelming. Grief is, in effect, merely a reflection of the love of the deceased that is felt by those who remain behind. Such grief may abate in its intensity over time, but I am not convinced that it ever completely goes away. The depth of love will always cause some degree of grief, even though it will become less acute over time.

The diminution of grief, as far as it can be assuaged, is made possible through the comforting embrace of the Holy Ghost and a fuller understanding of Heavenly Father's divine plan for the eternal destiny of His children. We are, after all, eternal beings. President Boyd K. Packer taught, "Mortal death is no more an ending than birth was a beginning."[51]

This relationship between the start and the end of mortal life was inspiringly encapsulated by the English poet William Wordsworth in his "Ode on Intimations of Immortality." Many can quote the beginning of the fifth stanza,

Our birth is but a sleep and a forgetting:
The Soul that rises with us, our Life's star,
Hath had elsewhere its setting,
And cometh from afar:
Not in entire forgetfulness,
And not in utter nakedness,
But trailing clouds of glory do we come,
From God, who is our home:
Heaven lies about us in our infancy![52]

Less often quoted are his words in the tenth stanza of the same poem, relating to death:

Though nothing can bring back the hour
Of splendor in the grass, of glory in the flower;
We will grieve not, rather find
Strength in what remains behind;
In the primal sympathy,
Which having been must ever be;
In the soothing thoughts that spring
Out of human suffering:
In the faith that looks through death.[53]

In effect, those who know and understand the central role of birth and death in mortality, have the conviction that the end of mortal life is merely the passing on to the next phase of our immortal lives. With that understanding, we do not believe in death.

As Elder Orson F. Whitney stated, "We are not going to die. We are deathless beings. We lived before we came into this world, and we shall live after we go out of it. What we call death is not worthy the name. There is no death for the righteous. Christ died to destroy death. The change called death is but a temporary separation of the spirit from the body. . . . None of our dear departed ones are dead. They have but gone before. This so-called death, when properly understood, is simply a going back home."[54]

Although a loved one has gone, the bereaved are not left entirely bereft. There are memories of good times, of loving embraces, of sterling achievements, and of last words. As Muriel Cuthbert, beloved wife of my mission president Elder Derek A. Cuthbert, was in her final hours, she mustered enough strength to say to her gathered family, "Endure to the end. I love you." These are words that will live in my memory forever. They not only epitomized her own life—full of love and devoted endurance to the end—they also stand as wonderful counsel to all who follow. As I think of her life, vitality, and many accomplishments, I will never forget this final lesson.

The Cuthbert family, and all of those who served as missionaries under the leadership of the Cuthberts, have blessed memories which overwhelm the grief of loss.

The power of memory was bravely set out by the British World War I poet Rupert Brooke in his own epitaph, which was also intended for all who lost their lives in the Great War.

> If I should die, think only this of me;
> That there's some corner of a foreign field
> That is for ever England. There shall be
> in that rich earth a richer dust concealed;
> a dust whom England bore, shaped, made aware,
> gave once, her flowers to love, her ways to roam,
> a body of England's breathing English air,
> Washed by the river, blest by suns of home.
>
> And think this heart, all evil shed away,
> A pulse in the eternal mind, no less
> Gives somewhere back the thoughts of England given;
> Her sights and sounds; dreams happy as her day;
> And laughter, learnt of friends; and gentleness
> In hearts at peace, under an English heaven.[55]

Rupert Brooke is buried in Greece.

The message is that the loss of a loved one in war can perhaps be assuaged by reflection on why the sacrifice was made: to save the country, and the world, from subjugation and tyranny. That the burial spot of those who gave their lives in battle for freedom is a blessed place as it represents the giving of one's life for a noble cause, a total act of selfless sacrifice. Hopefully some degree of peace, of coming to terms with the loss, is made possible by remembering why the sacrifice has been made in the first place. In recent years, many families in the United States, United Kingdom, and elsewhere have faced this reality with lives lost in Iraq, Afghanistan, and other trouble spots. "Remember this of me" is a message that says, "My life has not been given in vain."

In other settings, with grief of the more general kind, I believe there does come a time when happy memories begin to replace thoughts of sadness and loss: a memory of a life well lived, achievements made, and love given. Peace will come as thoughts of life, love, and goodness begin to dominate our days and nights.

The feeling of peace amidst death is also encouraged as we remember Heavenly Father's plan for the happiness of His children. Earth life and mortal death, are essential to that plan.

President Spencer W. Kimball explained, "The meaning of death has not changed. It releases a spirit for growth and development; and places a body in the repair shop of Mother Earth, there to be recast, remolded into a perfect body, an immortal glorious temple, clean and whole, perfected and ready for its occupant for eternity."[56]

The doctrinal position of the Church was clearly set out by Elder Bruce R. McConkie,

> We shouted for joy at the privilege of becoming mortal because without the tests of mortality there could be no eternal life. We now sing praises to the great Redeemer for the privilege of passing from this life because without death and the resurrection we could not be raised in immortal glory and gain eternal life. . . .
>
> Now, we do not seek death, though it is part of the merciful plan of the great Creator. Rather, we rejoice in life, and desire to live as long as we can be of service to our fellowmen. Faithful saints are a leaven of righteousness in a wicked world.[57]

It is well to now consider specific issues relating to the passing of loved ones.

Location of the Spirit World, and Those Who Die without the Law

President Brigham Young taught, "Where is the spirit world? It is right here. Do the good and evil spirits go together? Yes, they do. . . . Do they go to the sun? No. Do they go beyond the boundaries of this organized earth? No, they do not. They are brought forth upon this earth for the express purpose of inhabiting it to all eternity."[58]

Parley P. Pratt went further: "As to its location, it is here, . . . or, in other words, the earth and other planets of a like sphere, have their inward or spiritual spheres, as well as their outward, or temporal. The one is peopled by temporal tabernacles, and the other by spirits. A veil is drawn between the one sphere and another, whereby all the objects in the spiritual sphere are rendered invisible to those in the temporal."[59]

Revealed scripture states, "Man was also in the beginning with God. Intelligence, or the light of truth, was not created or made, neither indeed can be. All truth is independent in that sphere in which God has placed it, to act for itself, as all intelligence also; otherwise there is no existence" (Doctrine & Covenants 93:29–30).

We can therefore conclude that there is, in effect, a sphere within a sphere, a spirit world within our temporal world. There is work to be done there, as here, for the salvation of mankind. The righteous are gathered and organized to carry forth the teachings of the gospel to those who died without the law, and those who did not live worthy lives during mortality. Goodness, intelligence, awareness, love, gospel understanding, and priesthood power will remain with the spirits of the righteous, and the Lord will use them to good effect there, as He has done here.

Fate of Those without Gospel Knowledge

There are billions of Heavenly Father's children on earth who have never, nor will ever, hear the gospel of Jesus Christ in its fulness. What of them? Is there no hope? Traditional Christianity has no answer, but the restored truth does.

In a great, unparalleled, and selfless work, The Church of Jesus Christ of Latter-day Saints extends the hope and saving ordinances to all such individuals. Not content with work among the living, divine mandate has drawn members of the Church into the opportunities of salvation for the dead. In our temples, sacred, saving, and eternal ordinances are performed for those who have died "without the law." Of course, the proxy baptism and confirmation of such people does not make them members of the Church, nor are they included on Church membership records. This simply provides an opportunity for such people to enjoy the full blessings of eternal life, should they choose to accept the gospel in its fulness, for such an opportunity will be theirs in the spirit world.

We know that the gospel will be taught there, as well as on earth. After all, it is just the continuation of the work that was initiated by the Savior Himself. As the New Testament records: "For Christ also hath once suffered for sins, the just for the unjust, that he might bring us to God, being put to death in the flesh, but quickened by the Spirit: By which also he went and preached unto the spirits in Prison" (1 Peter 3:18–19).

Peter then declared: "For this cause was the gospel preached also to them that are dead, that they might be judged according to men in the flesh, but live according to God, in the spirit" (1 Peter 4:6).

In a revelation given to President Joseph F. Smith on October 3, 1918, just one month before the end of World War I, it is made clear that when Jesus went to the spirit world, in the three days betwixt His Crucifixion and Resurrection, "he organized his forces and appointed messengers, clothed with power and authority, and commissioned them to go forth and carry the light of the gospel to those that were in darkness, even to all the spirits of men; and thus was the gospel preached to the dead" (Doctrine & Covenants 138:30).

> The righteous spirit that departs from this earth is assigned its place in the paradise of God. It has its privileges and honors which are in point of excellency, far above and beyond human comprehension; and in this sphere of action, enjoying this partial reward for its righteous conduct on the earth, it continues its labors, and in this respect is very different from the state of the body from which it is released. For while the body sleeps and decays, the spirit receives a new birth; to it the petals of life are opened. It is born again into the presence of God.[60]

Entering the spirit world will be totally glorious. First, we leave behind the clay and dust of our physical beings: no more illness, disturbance, or fear. Our spirit body is released, with all of our earthly experience, intelligence, attitudes, and personality, but in a pure spiritual condition. Of course, our greatest progress is made when spirit and body are united. President Brigham Young taught, "I shall not cease learning while I live, nor when I arrive in the spirit-world; but shall then learn with greater facility; and when I again receive my body, I shall learn a thousand times more in a thousand times less time."[61] Modern revelation teaches, "For man is spirit. The elements are eternal, and spirit and element, inseparably connected, receive a fullness of joy; and when separated, man cannot receive a fullness of joy" (Doctrine & Covenants 93:33–34).

In the spirit world, despite the loss of our physical bodies, we will be able to accomplish a great work. Our "fulness of joy" will come when body and spirit are reunited after the glorious day of resurrection.

Meanwhile, if we are to emerge into that spiritual sphere described in scripture as "paradise," we need to have developed ourselves spiritually while on earth, exercised faith and devotion, and been obedient to the commandments of the Lord.

For those who were unrighteous on earth, their condition in the world of spirits is known as "spirit prison." The spirits of the righteous who labor in the spirit world will seek to rescue those whose condition is that of a prison. They will have success. Is this not a glorious, comforting confirmation of Heavenly Father's love for all of His children? It seems that the conditions for gospel acceptance will be favorable. President Lorenzo Snow confirmed, "I believe . . . that when the gospel is preached to the spirits in prison, the success attending that preaching will be far greater than that attending the preaching of our elders in this life. I believe there will be very few indeed of those spirits who will not gladly receive the gospel when it is carried to them." [62]

There can be a relationship between those who inhabit paradise in the spiritual sphere and those who remain in the mortal sphere. President Joseph F. Smith taught, "Our fathers and mothers, brothers, sisters, and friends who have passed away from this earth, having been faithful, and worthy to enjoy these rights and privileges, may have a mission given them to visit their relatives and friends upon the earth again, bringing from the divine Presence messages of love, of warning, of reproof and instruction to those whom they have learned to love in the flesh." [63]

Certainly death is not the end; were it so, "we are of all men most miserable" (1 Corinthians 15:19).

Our spirits are eternal. We existed before we came to earth, and will continue to exist when this earth life is over. As we enter the world of spirits, which is here on earth, albeit kept from our eyes in another sphere, we will be met by those we love who have gone before.

When I was speaking at my mother's funeral, the Holy Ghost made me aware that as she was slipping from the tearful embrace of her daughter Eileen, she was being welcomed by the joyful arms of her daughter Mary who had died in her infancy and for whom my mother secretly grieved all of her life.

I am also convinced that those who have gone before can be authorized to be ministering angels to loved ones still on earth. At times when we feel lifted from being downcast it may well be spiritual strength and encouragement from a loved one in the spirit world. A clear example of this was related by President David O McKay and retold by President Harold B. Lee.

A few weeks ago, President [David O.] McKay related to the Twelve an interesting experience, and I asked him yesterday if I might repeat it to you this morning.

He said it is a great thing to be responsive to the whisperings of the Spirit, and we know that when these whisperings come it is a gift and our privilege to have them. They come when we are relaxed and not under pressure of appointments. (I want you to mark that.) The President then took occasion to relate an experience in the life of Bishop John Wells, former member of the Presiding Bishopric.

A son of Bishop Wells was killed in Emigration Canyon on a railroad track. Brother John Wells was a great detail man and prepared many of the reports we are following up now. His boy was run over by a freight train. Sister Wells was inconsolable. She mourned during the three days prior to the funeral, received no comfort at the funeral, and was in a rather serious state of mind.

One day soon after the funeral services while she was lying on her bed relaxed but still mourning, she said her son appeared to her and said, "Mother, do not mourn, do not cry. I am all right." He told her that she did not understand how the accident happened and explained that he had given the signal to the engineer to move on, and then made the usual effort to catch the railing on the freight train; but as he attempted to do so his foot caught on a root and he failed to catch the handrail, and his body fell under the train. It was clearly an accident.

Now, listen. He said that as soon as he realized that he was in another environment he tried to see his father, but couldn't reach him. His father was so busy with the duties in his office he could not respond to his call. Therefore he had come to his mother. He said to her, "You tell Father that all is well with me, and I want you not to mourn anymore."

Then the President made the statement that the point he had in mind was that when we are relaxed in a private room we are more susceptible to those things; and that so far as he was concerned, his best thoughts come after he gets up in the morning and is relaxed and thinking about the duties of the day; that impressions come more clearly, as if it were to hear a voice. Those impressions are right. If we are worried and upset about something, the inspiration does not come. If we so live that our minds are free from worry and our conscience is clear and our feelings are right toward one another, the operation of the Spirit of the Lord upon our spirit is as real as when we pick up the telephone; but when they come, we must be brave enough to take the suggested actions.[64]

Although there have been a limited number of recorded experiences, most of these instances of ethereal support would be so personally sacred that they would not and should not be shared more widely.

While meeting with priesthood leaders in Santa Fe, New Mexico, one of our valiant men stood up and asked if he could share such an experience which he said had happened to him in the temple. I quietly suggested to him that perhaps that was so sacred that it should remain with him and not be spoken of openly. He nodded his head and sat down again. I believe that there are probably many instances of a blessing being received by one on earth as a result of an assignment given to a loved one in the spirit world, but that they would be too personally sacred to be spoken of openly or even recorded.

We do not fear death: we welcome our entry into the supernal sphere known as the spirit world. This life is not all there is; we are not mere mortals. Life does not end with death, we simply move on to the next appointment. We need not be balefully bereft when a mortal life ends; we can and should feel magnificently blessed that our loved one truly is in a better place, surrounded by those who have gone before, with a heavenly mission to perform: to rescue the "captives."

The concepts here expressed can be summarized in a few sentences: There is life beyond death. It is real, sweet, and almost tangible. There is a world of spirits. When our mortal life ends, we go "back home," to await the glorious resurrection. In the grief that comes with the passing of a loved one, be at peace; the book of life is not yet finished. Rejoice!

Suicide

When a family member commits suicide, it is even more gut-wrenching for those who are left behind. The devastation that results is truly awful. Family members are left to cope, not just with bereavement, but also with nagging, hollow feelings of guilt. They desperately worry and wonder what they could have done to prevent it. Their peace is totally disturbed and is hard to regain. Usually, there is not much that could have been done by anyone.

It is believed that some suicide attempts are attention seeking, but one can never be sure. My mother's second husband fell into this manipulative category on more than one event, and he spent some time in a psychiatric facility; it was all very disturbing.

Who can properly tell or fathom why, how, or when someone reaches so far into the pit of depression that their mental and emotional distress reaches a point where they are running on empty; when death seems more desirable than life?

The position of the Church in relation to this is clearly set out in a policy statement in the Church *Handbook of Instructions*.

> It is wrong to take a life, including one's own. However, a person who commits suicide may not be responsible for his or her acts. Only God can judge such a matter.
>
> The family, in consultation with the bishop, determines the place and nature of a funeral service. . . . Church facilities may be used. If the person was endowed, he or she may be buried in temple clothing.[65]

Death of the Young

The loss of a young family member, who passes to the spirit world, can be especially heartbreaking. However, Joseph Smith taught, "The only difference between the old and young dying is, one lives longer in heaven and eternal light and glory than the other, and is freed a little sooner from this miserable wicked world."[66]

President Spencer W. Kimball wrote, "If we say that early death is a calamity, disaster or tragedy, would it not be saying that mortality is preferable to earlier entrance into the spirit world and eventual salvation and exaltation? If mortality be the perfect state, then death would be a frustration, but the gospel teaches us, 'There is no tragedy in death, but only in sin . . . blessed are the dead that die in the Lord.'"[67]

For those in the world who are not blessed with knowledge of restored truth of our eternal nature, the death of a young person can be desperately devastating, totally tragic, and utterly unbearable, with the loss considered miserably meaningless. They can often find no consoling comfort, no sense of perfect peace.

Many in such a position have received little comfort from the ministers of "Traditional Christianity," especially if a child dies without being christened or baptized. My mother-in-law faced this situation when she lost twin stillborn boys. Her priest explained that because these boys had not been baptized, they would go to a place called "limbo," neither heaven nor hell, where they would remain for eternity. Uncomforted, unsure if this was right, she went to her husband's minister to ask the same question, "What happens to my boys who did not live long enough to be christened?" His reply was equally without healing hope. "We do not know, it is just one of the mysteries of God."

Finding no comfort from these statements, she decided that she would no longer have anything to do with any church.

Then, some seven years later, two of the Lord's missionaries knocked on her door. Although she still had no interest in organized religion, she invited them in for respite from the bitterly cold snow. When the missionaries were eventually told of the heart-felt issue, they simply turned to the Book of Mormon: Another Testament of Jesus Christ, to share the truth; "Little children are alive in Christ, even from the foundation of the world. . . . He that supposeth that little children need baptism is in the gall of bitterness and in the bonds of iniquity" (Moroni 8:12, 14). Further, "Little children need no repentance, neither baptism" (Moroni 8:11).

In contrast to the false doctrine, which brought darkness and no comfort, the true gospel of Jesus Christ brought light and knowledge, comfort, hope, and peace.

Gospel perspective can turn night to day, darkness into light, misery to joy, distress to love, and loss to hope. For the bereaved, peace is available through the doctrine of Christ and the shedding forth of the consoling comfort of the Holy Ghost.

My mother-in-law bore two more children, one of whom I had the good fortune to marry.

The eternal truth is, "Little children need no baptism," for they are "alive in Christ."

It does seem that some die in infancy, as Joseph Smith explained, "That they may escape the envy of man and the sorrows and evils of this present world; they were too pure, too lovely, to live on earth."[68]

President Joseph Fielding Smith taught that, "Children who die in childhood will not be deprived of any blessing. When they grow, after the resurrection, to the full maturity of the spirit, they will be entitled to all the blessings which they would have been entitled to had they been privileged to tarry here and receive them."[69]

Speaking to a grieving mother, Joseph Smith promised, "You will have the joy, the pleasure, and satisfaction of nurturing this child, after its resurrection, until it reaches the full stature of its spirit."[70]

Some lose faith, lose their way, and lose all feelings of hope and peace when tragedy strikes. Prayerful blessings sometimes seem to be ignored. With inspirational insight, President Spencer W. Kimball taught,

> Now we find many people critical when a righteous person is killed, or a young father or mother is taken from a family, or when violent deaths occur. Some become bitter when oft-repeated prayers seem unanswered. Some lose faith and turn sour when solemn administrations by holy men seem to be ignored and no restoration seems to come from repeated prayer circles. But if all the sick were healed, if all the righteous were protected and the wicked destroyed, the whole program of the Father would be annulled and the basic principle of the gospel, free agency, would be ended.
>
> If pain and sorrow and total punishment immediately followed the doing of evil, no soul would repeat a misdeed. If joy and peace and rewards were instantaneously given the doer of good, there would be no evil—all would do good and not because of the righteousness of doing good. There would be no test of strength, no free agency, no Satanic controls.
>
> Should all prayers be immediately answered according to our selfish desires and our limited understanding, then there would be little or no suffering, sorrow, disappointment, or even death; and if these were not, there would also be an absence of joy, success, resurrection, eternal life, and godhood.[71]

Although the miracles we seek and pray for may not come, others may be ours. A few years ago, President Monson's office passed to me an assignment to visit and give a blessing to a young man in response to a letter the President had received making such a request. The young man, not long married and whose wife was pregnant with a young boy due in a few months, had severe leukemia, and several treatments had failed. It seemed that he did not have long to live. I gave him a priesthood blessing in which the Lord told him he would live to hold his newborn son in his arms and give him a father's blessing.

We were all surprised, including me. It was one of those occasions when the Holy Ghost prompts you to say something and you find yourself saying it, and then upon getting home afterward, praying earnestly and pleading that the blessing would be fulfilled. Well, he did not die at that point, but was still alive as the time approached for the birth. Circumstances were so arranged that he was taken into the delivery room, and he witnessed the birth of his son, and held him in his arms. Local priesthood leaders then organized privately and quickly for this very ill new father to bless and name his boy.

A short time later, as this young father's life was fading fast, I visited him, now at home, surrounded by his family. I held his baby son in my arms and felt his father's total love for him. It was all a miracle, even though the good brother did not live. That miracle did not happen because it was not meant to happen. Nevertheless, a miracle did occur, in the preservation of his life so that this good father could at least see and bless his son.

President Joseph F. Smith wrote,

> I am looking forward to the time when I have passed away from this stage of existence, there I shall be permitted to enjoy more fully every gift and blessing that have contributed to my happiness in the world; everything. I do not believe that there is one thing that was designed or intended to give me joy or make me happy, that I shall be denied hereafter, provided I continue faithful; otherwise my joy cannot be full. I am not speaking of the happiness or pleasure that is derived from sin; I refer to the happiness experienced in seeking to do the will of God on earth as it is done in heaven. We expect to have our wives and husbands in eternity. I expect this; I look for nothing else. Without it, I should not be happy. The thought or belief that I should be denied this privilege hereafter would make me miserable from this moment.[72]

While waiting for a flight from Samoa to New Zealand I introduced myself to a leader of another faith who was making the same trip. I intended to simply exchange pleasantries. Unfortunately, he would rather have had an argument focused on temple work. He demanded to know the doctrinal reason for spending all "this money" on temples. I then spoke of eternal marriage and his response was to quote the scripture when the Savior, responding to a question, said after the resurrection "they neither marry, nor are given in marriage" (Mark 12:25).

When I shared the insight that for marriage to be eternal it had to be sealed on earth, not after the resurrection, he was not convinced by my "convenient explanation." I commented that for me, heaven would not be heaven if my wife, the love of my life, was not there with me; whereupon his wife who was standing next to him said, "I agree with you; that is what I think too." The conversation came to a rapid end. I thought afterward, of this verse from a favorite hymn:

> How great, how glorious, how complete
> Redemption's grand design,
> Where justice, love, and mercy meet
> In harmony divine![73]

Heavenly Father's divine plan for the eternal happiness of all His children is indeed great, glorious, and complete. It is the grand design of redemption.

Death is not final, it is not terminal; it is simply the door through which we must pass to enter into the next stage, the next sphere, of our eternal existence. Because of Jesus Christ, there is no sting in death; the grave is denied a victory. As is testified in an uplifting hymn, "Death is conquered; man is free. Christ has won the victory."[74]

Knowing the eternal nature of man and woman, and having an understanding of "Redemption's grand design," changes our sense of loss from night to day. It is what brings calm to the mind, solace to the heart, and peace to the soul.

CHAPTER 6

Peaceful Places

$\mathcal{F}$inding peace often necessitates finding places of peace: environments where the Holy Ghost can whisper peace to our souls. In modern revelation, as both a promise and an instruction, the Lord said, "My disciples shall stand in holy places" (Doctrine & Covenants 45:32). Holy places are also peaceful places. This chapter explores those places where we can find peace.

The Temple

Each and every sacred temple is an oasis of peace. Within the walls of a temple we experience the "perfect mildness" that is promised through the Holy Ghost. Celestial serenity flows from celestial service. Although we often hear the expression "taking out one's endowment," it is a significant misnomer. The term "take out" applies to fast food restaurants, not the ordinances of the temple. We do not "take out" our endowment, *we receive it*. The temple endowment blesses us with the gift of peace and eternal experience. Many of those who are not members of the Church but who nonetheless visit an open house prior to the dedication of a temple, comment on the peace they feel within its walls.

Temple furnishings are exquisite; they represent the best that can be provided to assist in elevating our thinking, and are such that befits a "house of the Lord." However, the Holy Ghost and the endowment blessings are not found in the beautiful crystal chandeliers or in the lovely soft furnishings, but in the holy ordinances. What really matters is that once a temple is dedicated, the Holy Ghost comes as the Holy Spirit of Promise to ratify ordinances and bless the people with peace. Thus we read in the Old Testament of events pertaining to Solomon's temple, that "the cloud filled the house of the Lord . . . for the glory of the Lord had filled the house of the Lord" (1 Kings 8:10–11). Given that each temple is a sacred place of peace, we feel apart from the tumult of the world whenever we cross its threshold; and we speak in hushed voices, whispers even.

We are blessed to live in a day when temples are spreading across the earth. Like droplets of golden rain from heaven, temples are bringing refreshment to nations and peoples. Little wonder that every new temple that is announced brings joy and godly feeling to members of the Church in these lands. It is all akin to the response of the people who had recently returned from captivity when the foundation of Zerubbabel's temple was laid. Scripture records that

> they sang together by course in praising and giving thanks unto the Lord; because he is good, for his mercy endureth for ever toward Israel. And all the people shouted with a great shout, when they praised the Lord, because the foundation of the house of the Lord was laid.
>
> But many of the priests and Levites and chiefs of the fathers, who were ancient men, that had seen the first house, when the foundation of this house was laid before their eyes, wept with a loud voice; and many shouted aloud for joy:
>
> So that the people could not discern the noises of the shout of joy from the noise of the weeping of the people. (Ezra 3:11–13)

This is a lovely description of the emotions of our people when a temple is announced, a foundation laid, and when the house of the Lord is dedicated. All are filled with joy and gladness, some simply weep.

The degradation and destruction of the world fades somewhat in the face of the construction of these holy places of peace. The "golden rain" brings light and life to the desolation that has gripped the world. In the place of dereliction of divine moral values currently sweeping across the earth like a toxic rash, each temple reaches heavenward, and demonstrates that there can be hope, peace, and freedom from degradation. Little wonder that Elder George Q. Cannon said, "Every foundation stone that is laid for a temple, and every temple completed . . . lessens the power of Satan on the earth."[75]

We know from the New Testament that Jesus at times found it necessary to be alone to meditate. We read that "he went up into a mountain apart to pray: and when the evening was come, he was there alone" (Matthew 14:23). The Apostle John confirms that Jesus, "departed again into a mountain himself alone" (John 6:15). He left the multitude to allow quiet solitude to reflect and commune with the Father. So must we. Such peaceful stillness that we find in the temple provides the opportunity for reflection, for drawing ourselves close to heaven, and reminds us of the promise of eternal glory.

Perhaps we lose sight, somewhat, of the divine peace that we find in the temple when we refer to "temple work," or "ordinance workers," when what we do in the temple is less about work and more about sublime service.

A former president of the Nuku'alofa Tonga Temple, Sione Fineangonofo, related an experience he had one day in the temple. He noticed that a young child had been left by herself in the foyer of the temple while her mother completed some proxy ordinances. When the mother returned, he gently reminded her that the temple is not a nursery, and that her daughter should not have been left by herself. This dear mother responded, "Oh, she was not alone; the sister I was representing was looking after her." This good mother was at peace because she recognized the divine nature of what is done within the walls of temples.

Of course, this experience should not imply that parents should leave their children in the waiting room of a temple to be watched over by heavenly beings as they do temple work. The message of this story and the reason for its inclusion is simply to illustrate that there are supernal experiences to be had in the Lord's temples.

While serving in the temple, I have also gained peace from revelation. When I was first called to serve as a bishop I was twenty-five and frankly did not know very much. The average age of ward members was well over twice my age. My mother and three teenage sisters were members of the ward. I had not told them of the call, so it was a complete surprise. When my name was announced, there was an audible gasp from my sisters at the shock of realization that during their teenage years their bishop would be their brother, and my mother said, "Oh no" out loud. Their responses were a fair reflection on how I felt. I knew I was desperately in need of the Lord's help, especially given that this was His work, and I felt that He would do some of it. I also knew that my assignment was to represent His will to the people, not the other way around. In effect, I had to get my "marching orders" from Him.

As we read in Proverbs, "Trust in the Lord with all thine heart; and lean not unto thine own understanding. In all thy ways acknowledge him, and he shall direct thy paths" (Proverbs 3:5–6).

So I knew I needed the Lord's help, and I sought it through prayer. Day after day, hour after hour, I prayed inwardly and vocally to gain an understanding of what He would have me do, what mission He desired me to fulfill. Nothing came; the heavens seemed closed. By the end of the week I was beginning to think that I should not have been called, that He was rejecting me. I added fasting to my prayers and then visited the temple in London, England. In those days, the London England Temple had one large ordinance room with a balcony usually occupied by the brethren; it would usually take some time to pass through to the celestial room. While I was waiting, I continued to pray about my assignment. I received a flood of revelation in which the Lord told me what to do, specific names were even mentioned. As described by Joseph Smith, this was "pure intelligence" that seemed to flow through my whole body. I knew what I had been called to do. I was at peace. Since then I have always retired to the temple whenever I have sought such direction or confirmation. The feelings of peace have continued over the years. I consider the temple to be the ultimate sanctuary of peace.

The Sacrament Table

Each week we have the opportunity to sit reverently in a sacrament meeting to ponder, reflect, and feel. Of course, the sacrament was instituted by the Savior during the Last Supper, the eve of the final day of His mortal life. Watching over those who later would prove unable to watch but one hour with Him (see Matthew 26:40), His deep desire was to forever bless those who were to bear special witness of His name in all the world. He then knelt to wash their feet.

Then, His hands reach out to touch the bread and lift the cup as, in solemn stillness, He offers them as symbols of His life and mission. Simplicity saturated with supreme significance. This sacramental supper was intended as the means by which His disciples in ages to come would remember Him, and in so doing overcome the world.

From His lips falls a powerful discourse (see John 14:15–16), and then an exquisite, intimate prayer of intercession, a prayer not for Himself, despite the dreadful anticipation of the agonies that He would personally have to bear, but for His apostles and for all the saints. He pleads that they—we—might find joy in Him, be kept from evil, and "be sanctified through the spirit" (John 17:13–20).

Centuries have passed and we, as disciples of Christ across the nations of the earth, enjoy the privilege of remembering that sacramental scene. Each week, as we meet to partake of the sacrament, we are given the opportunity to specifically remember the Savior. This precious time when we sit as "fellow citizens with the Saints, and of the household of God" (Ephesians 2:19) allows for quiet reflection, personal introspection, spiritual renewal—what Elder L. Tom Perry has described as "a sacred moment in a holy place."[76] It is a time for contemplation and commitment.

Somehow, we must make sure that such an experience, although regularly familiar, never becomes simply routine and incidental to our Sunday worship. Partaking of the sacrament in remembrance of the Savior is not incidental to our sacrament meetings or our Sabbath days. It is the very reason why the sacrament meeting is held; it is all else that takes place that is supportive of the sacred, sacramental experience. As Elder Russell M. Nelson has taught, the sacrament "is the highlight of our Sabbath day observance."[77]

Taking the sacrament is the only priesthood ordinance that we have the privilege of repeating for ourselves every week. The Lord intends it to be a principal means whereby "Thou mayest more fully keep thyself unspotted from the world" (Doctrine & Covenants 59:9). I wonder if this is how we individually think when we partake of the sacrament each week. Are we there just for the talks and music, as uplifting as we hope they will be? We must remember that we are principally there to experience a sacred sacrament.

The Apostle Paul testified that when Jesus instituted the sacrament He instructed, "This do in remembrance of me" (1 Corinthians 11:24. See also verses 23–30).

So, in our sacramental prayers we confirm to Heavenly Father that, as the prayers proclaim, we eat the bread "in remembrance of the body of thy Son," and we drink the water "in remembrance of the blood of thy Son." We then acknowledge and witness that "[we] do always remember him" (See Doctrine & Covenants 20:75–79).

President Joseph F. Smith taught that Jesus provided the sacrament as a law "by which His life and mission, His death and resurrection, the great sacrifice He had offered for the redemption of man, should be kept in everlasting remembrance."[78]

Such remembrance like prayer, "is the Christian's vital breath."[79] Johann Richter wrote, "Remembrance is the only paradise out of which we cannot be driven away."[80] So, when we take the sacrament each week, we remember.

We remember the prophetic pronouncement of His life and mission that preceded His mortal birth: "For unto us a child is born, unto us a son is given: and the government shall be upon his shoulder: and his name shall be called Wonderful, Counselor, The mighty God, The everlasting Father, The Prince of Peace" (Isaiah 9:6).

We remember the joyful anthem of the heavenly host proclaiming at His birth, "Glory to God in the highest, and on earth peace, good will toward men" (Luke 2:14).

We remember His earthly ministry—the parables, the miracles, the divine teachings of true doctrine, the principles and ordinances that constitute the good news of His gospel—and we renew our commitment to "lay hold upon the gospel of Christ" (Mormon 7:8).

We remember His precious Atonement, reflecting as best we can on the anguish of Gethsemane, the darkness of Calvary, and the glorious dawn of Resurrection day, knowing that He "offereth himself a sacrifice for sin, to answer the ends of the law, unto all those who have a broken heart and a contrite spirit" (2 Nephi 2:7). We repent and change, for we know that no unclean thing can enter into His presence, and, as President Marion G. Romney testified, "to return into that presence becomes the supreme faith and hope of [our] existence."[81]

We remember the blessings of the Restoration of truth and authority following years of apostasy, the coming forth of the Book of Mormon, the establishment of The Church of Jesus Christ of Latter-day Saints, and the purpose of it all which is "to bear testimony of mine Only Begotten; his resurrection from the dead; yea, and also the resurrection of all men; and righteousness and truth will I cause to sweep the earth as with a flood, to gather out mine elect from the four quarters of the earth" (Moses 7:62). We think of our role in this great cause and strengthen our resolve to do our part.

We remember the eternal nature of families and of our

responsibilities to those we love, recognizing that such relationships are central to Heavenly Father's plan for our happiness and to the Savior's mission, "and all this that the earth might answer the end of its creation" (Doctrine & Covenants 49:16).

We remember His invitation to "come unto Christ, and be perfected in Him, and deny yourselves of all ungodliness . . . and love God with all your might, mind and strength" (Moroni 10:32), and we pledge ourselves anew to "be risen with Christ, [to] seek those things which are above," and to set our "affection on things above, not on things on the earth" (Colossians 3:1–2).

President Joseph Fielding Smith explained, "To always remember him does not mean simply to remember that He was crucified, but to keep in mind constantly the reasons why, and what blessings have come to each of us through his death and resurrection. We are to remember the great suffering and what it cost him to make the great atonement. We are to remember that He did it because of His love, not only for those who believe on Him, but also for the whole world."[82]

All of this is what we remember as we take the blessed bread and as the sacramental water passes our lips. Our desire and commitment, even the very covenant we make, is to engage in such intimate remembrance not just in our formal sacrament meetings, but always.

When kneeling at a sacred altar with the one you love, remember Him.

As you hold a newborn child in your arms, remember Him.

At the graveside of a loved one, remember Him.

In times of testing trial and moments of exhilarating success, remember Him.

When surrounded by the darkness of temptation, remember Him.

In the midst of pain and doubts, anxiety and loneliness, remember Him.

In cloud and in sunshine, remember Him.

I would urge that you remember Him always, and I testify that He always remembers you.

If we are to fully gain the sense of heavenly peace that comes from partaking of the sacrament, we would do well to fully participate in every aspect of the ordinance. This includes singing the sacrament hymn, even if we feel we cannot sing—after all, we are participating in a worship service, not auditioning for the Tabernacle Choir. This includes listening quietly to the prayers, reflecting on their content, and inwardly recommitting ourselves to the covenants we have already made. This includes listening to the quiet whisperings of the Holy Ghost, and recognizing the significance of it all as we reverently take the bread and the water.

It is my observation that engaging in other distracting activities, including using cell phones, texting, messaging, and chewing gum during the singing and the prayers are out of keeping with and are demeaning to this sacred experience. After all, the promise to us, as contained in modern revelation, is that "[by offering] up thy sacraments upon my holy day," we will be able to "more fully keep [ourselves] unspotted from the world" (Doctrine & Covenants 59:9).

As we do this "with thanksgiving, with cheerful hearts and countenances" (Doctrine & Covenants 59:15) and give respect to the rest of the Lord's day, we are further promised that "the fullness of the earth is [ours]" (Doctrine & Covenants 59:16).

Of course, it is recognized that parents with young children may have to attend to them instead of sitting quietly without distraction. It is for each parent to determine how to cope with this whilst still gaining the blessings promised to those who "offer up thy sacraments." There is no easy or all-embracing answer to this; parents can only do the best they can, without feelings of guilt.

Keeping ourselves "unspotted from the world" will prove to be a great enhancer of peace. I venture to suggest that this is second only to temple service in providing a peaceful place in which we find stillness, calmness, and consoling comfort.

Secret Prayer

An inspiring Church hymn, "Secret Prayer," begins with the words, "There is an hour of peace and rest, unmarred by earthly care; 'tis when before the Lord I go and kneel in secret prayer."[83]

When we find a private place, to be alone and pray, we do obtain the "hour of peace and rest." I have found it helpful to prepare in advance by inwardly singing a favorite hymn that points my thoughts to the Savior, or reading a pertinent scripture, then picturing Him in my mind, as far as I am able to do so, and then speaking softly but directly and reverently. All of this connects me with heaven and allows my prayer to be guided by the Holy Ghost. At the end of the prayer it has also proved helpful to quietly listen to and feel the promptings received. I have found it best to focus more on those things for which I am grateful and to confine requests mainly on behalf of others. I often pray in this manner while in my office during the day.

While I served as a missionary in Scotland, I met a good man who was receiving the missionary lessons. A telecommunications engineer by trade, he was quite practical and not necessarily given to spiritual things. One day while driving through a Scottish glen, radio reception of his favorite classical music channel began to break up. Uncharacteristically, he began to skip through other channels until he found one for which the reception was clear. It was a documentary-style report on the subject of Mormon pioneers who had crossed the American plains to find a home "far away in the West."[84]

He recalls being impressed by the comment that as they made their way across the United Saints, those who were in the forefront laid seeds for those who followed to harvest. He thought that this was a remarkable and selfless act of love. Later that week, while watching television (which this "higher thinking" man seldom did) he found himself viewing a BBC documentary about the Church.

Having listened to the radio program, he was impressed to watch the documentary; twice in the same week his interest in the Church was piqued. To insert a personal note at this point, I viewed this documentary in the company of investigators—we had been encouraged to do so—and I felt it was awful. Yet, it did not have such an effect on this good man.

The following day, two of the Lord's missionaries knocked on his door; because of the interest that had been aroused, he invited them in, and they began teaching him and his wife. When the missionaries invited him to be baptized, he knew he could only do it if he received for himself a spiritual confirmation that this gospel was true, and that this church truly was the Church of Jesus Christ.

To gain such a witness, and unknown to either the missionaries or his wife, he decided he had to pray in a place of solitude. He retired to the local Corstophine Hill, knelt, and prayed. He had to repeat this process several times before the answer came. He heard the response, "yes," and was filled with peace from the Holy Ghost. Shortly thereafter, he and his wife were baptized and confirmed. He has since served as a bishop, stake president, and as a counselor in the presidency of the

Scotland Edinburgh Mission. For him, "secret prayer" brought revelatory confirmation that he should become a member of the Church, and he has remained faithful ever since.

Prayer works, and secret prayer brings peace and rest.

As we seek out and put ourselves in peaceful places, so we are filled with peace. I have mentioned the temple, the sacrament table, and personal secret prayer as three such places; I invite the reader to consider the peaceful places that are available to him or her, and then to occupy such places often.

CHAPTER 7

Peaceful Pathways

However troubled our life may be, we can obtain perfect, personal peace. It is available to all, and it is achievable.

To one who is at peace, the world and their relationships take on a more positive hue; everything just looks different, their windows on the world reflect valuable vision and virtuous vistas.

This chapter begins to chart "peaceful pathways" to life that are both more peaceful and serene. They reflect lifestyle concepts.

Take Time to Be Still

Some time ago while sitting on an airplane waiting for other passengers to file on, a young boy age seven or so came on board and instantly demanded of the cabin crew, "Do you have Wi-Fi on this plane?" His parents did not bat an eyelid.

I reflected on the dismal state of our modern world when a child, with urgency, impatience, and arrogance, speaks to an adult in this way about his seemingly desperate need for a communications facility. Those of us from a slightly older generation lived in an entirely different world—not only in terms of technology, but even in the opportunity for air travel, which was extremely rare. Luxury travel generally took the form of a train, coach, or car. Today these opportunites are commonplace, but I am not sure that our peace has been enhanced very much by the hurly-burly of rushing from place to place by the fastest means possible.

It is interesting to see very small children rushing through teeming airport terminals, weighed down with backpacks and pulling little roller bags behind them, while their parents call on them to "hurry up," "keep up," or "get a move on." We seem to be anxious to indoctrinate children, at an ever younger age, with a sense of always having to be "on the go."

Adults continue, swamping airports with constant impatience. Elsewhere, they demand staccato, sound bite, streaming news. They drive on freeways as if on a race track, and have an insatiable demand for constant communications with cell phones that seem to require surgical removal. We appear to seldom have time just to stop, to be still, and to take time to breathe.

One of the results of this busy, noisy, and crammed world is an apparent increase in the modern malaise of "stress," the descriptor for many emotional and mental disorders. In many employment situations it is not only accepted, but even expected, that employees will prove their worth by total devotion to the company or organization, often at the sacrifice of home and family. Work is no longer confined to the office; instead the office is brought to the home, filling many evenings and weekends. Psychologist, therapists, doctors, and counselors are not short of work in addressing the effects of all of this.

A popular song of recent years made the claim, "Love is all around us . . . everywhere we go." It would perhaps be appropriate to now sing, "Noise is all around us, everywhere we go."

Even in the Church, local priesthood leaders and mission presidents find themselves involved in counseling those who have been caught up in the chains of noise-filled stress.

In my business life I made it a personal rule never to take work home, and I made sure everyone in my team knew that this was not expected of them; nor did I view any of them working late in the night as a "badge of honor."

Of course, rest from work has been made rather more difficult as a result of constant emails, although I have to say that quick email communications are preferable to time-wasting meetings, and can save time by exchanging information and decisions quickly. Much Church communication could be taken care of via emails midweek rather than becoming an occupation during Sunday meetings.

I also made it a personal habit, after a two-and-a-half-hour drive home from my office in London, just to sit quietly in the car for a few moments before crossing the threshold, in an attempt to put the fast and furious proceedings of the day to one side before greeting my family. I was not always successful in doing so, but it helped to spread peace whenever I did it. When I drove into work, I listened to the recording of the wartime speeches of Winston Churchill to be ready for the fray; going home required something altogether more peace inducing, usually classical music.

Somehow and in some way, in the midst of this avaricious attack on our sense of calm and peace, we each have to simply find the time, and a place of solitude to reflect, ponder, and "be still."

We may need to be more disciplined in finding the "power off" button on cell phones, televisions, computer terminals, and game consoles. We may need to travel less, or to make enough time available so that travel is not rushed.

For me, spending time by the sea and watching the ocean has proven to be a tranquil experience. When I was a boy, one of the residential homes I was sent to for respite from calamitous circumstances at home was "Castle Toward" near Dunoon in Scotland, situated in the Cowal Peninsula in Argyll. This was a nineteenth-century country home set in a marvelous estate very close to the sea. Whenever I could, I would sit or stand at the large, sashed windows just looking at the sea. A United States naval base was nearby in the Holy Loch, and Polaris submarines would often pass serenely along. On the too few occasions when I could go down to the shore, I would sit on a rocky outcrop looking out across the ocean, watching the waves ripple along. It was very therapeutic, comforting, and peaceful. It was bliss.[85]

We each can, and must find our own "places of peace," our own "times of tranquility." I venture to suggest that we are unlikely to ever feel real peace unless we make the time to simply "stand still."

Look Up

It is hard to feel a sense of peace if we are forever looking downward and are downcast. Looking upward to light, sky, and sunshine is far better for our emotional health than slouching down and gazing, as it were, at the ditch or the drain.

Of course, we can and do experience disturbance of our peace through internal and external agonies. Life is sometimes just plain hard; after all, it was meant to be. The crucible of affliction through which we each must pass can be soul stretching and robust; but in the midst of it all we can be shaped and purified, made more fit for the future and for life eternal.

There is a remarkable account told of a Sunday School class that was discussing the fate of the Martin and Willie handcart companies, which met with terrible tragedy because of their late, poorly provisioned start on the trek to the Salt Lake Valley.

> There was some sharp criticism of the leadership who did not prevent this from happening. Then, an elderly man rose and said,
>
> "I ask you to stop this criticism. You are discussing a matter you know nothing about. Cold, historic facts . . . give no proper interpretation of the question involved. A mistake to send the handcart company out so late in the season—Yes. But I was in that company and my wife too . . . we suffered beyond anything you can imagine and many died of exposure and starvation, but . . . we became acquainted with [God] in our extremities.
>
> "I have pulled my handcart when I was so weak and weary from illness and lack of food that I could hardly put one foot ahead of the other. I have looked ahead and seen a patch of sand or a hill slope and I have said, I can go only that far and there I must give up, for I cannot pull the load through it. I have gone to that sand, and when I reached it, the cart began pushing me. I have looked back many times to see who was pushing my cart, but my eyes saw no one. I knew then that the angels of God were there.
>
> "Was I sorry that I chose to come by handcart? No. The price we paid to become acquainted with God was a privilege to pay, and I am thankful that I was privileged to come in the Martin Handcart Company."
>
> The speaker was Francis Webster, and when he sat down there was not a dry eye in the room. We were a subdued and chastened lot. Charles Mabey, who later became governor of Utah, arose and voiced the sentiment of all when he said, "I would gladly pay the same price for the same assurance of eternal verities that Brother Webster has."[86]

Narrating the story of Francis Webster, President James E. Faust said: "In the heroic effort of the handcart pioneers, we learn a great truth. All must pass through a refiner's fire, and the insignificant and unimportant in our lives can melt away like dross and make our faith bright, intact, and strong. There seems to be a full measure of anguish, sorrow, and often heartbreak for everyone, including those who earnestly seek to do right and be faithful. Yet this is part of the purging to become acquainted with God."[87]

President David O. McKay taught, "The soul is the fountain from which the peace of the world will spring. Centered in the heart also are the enemies to peace—'avarice, ambition, envy, anger, and pride.'"[88]

Our perspective and view of life will change when, rather than being cast down, we look up.

Generally speaking, we are better than we think we are. Elder Neal A. Maxwell observed, "Some of us stand before no more harsh a judge than ourselves, a judge who stubbornly refuses to admit much happy evidence, and who cares nothing for due process."[89]

Elder Maxwell was spot on. Some of us do, indeed, stand before no more harsh a judge than ourselves. In a world of instant action replay of sports games, we often fall foul of the tendency to replay over and over again memories of our mistakes, our failures, our dreams dashed, our ambitions unfulfilled—every one of our dark experiences. It is dreadfully debilitating. If only we could do the same with our successes, our achievements, the "sunny spots" of our lives—dreams realized, ambitions fulfilled, all that we have been blessed with—and there will be many if we list them one-by-one.

Frankly, in the "Court of Personal Opinion" we often err gravely by only allowing evidence from the prosecution, never giving the defense a chance to make its argument or present its case.

Some things also take time to work out. Not everything can be accomplished straight away, even if we do live in an environment that is fast and falsely inviting. The cult of celebrity with all of its "tinsel town" trappings of unproductive lives has invaded our peace, presenting a fantasy world in which prizes come without paying the price. That is not the real world. That is not how the economy of heaven works.

Live to Serve

President Ezra Taft Benson gave the assurance, "To press on in noble endeavors, even while surrounded by a cloud of depression, will eventually bring you out on top into the sunshine."[90]

It has been said that we should live to serve and serve to live. The Savior put it this way, "For whosoever will save his life shall lose it: but whosoever will lose his life for my sake, the same shall save it" (Luke 9:24).

There is a great, transforming truth that when we live to lift the burdens of others, our own burdens become lighter. Although circumstances may not change, our attitude does. We are able to face our own trials with greater acceptance, a more understanding heart, and deeper gratitude for what we have, rather than persistent pining for what we yet lack.

In powerful phraseology, Paul counseled the Ephesians to "let no corrupt communication proceed out of your mouth, but that which is good to the use of edifying, that it may minister grace unto the hearers" (Ephesians 4:29).

This is a wonderful, mind-expanding concept. I am not sure that there is anything of more benefit to others that we could do than to "minister grace." In other words, to help them feel the peaceful uplifting grace of the Savior. That is an inspiring personal mission in life: to lift others through our words, but also by our actions.

It has been interesting to me to note that my own sense of melancholy and emotional disturbance through a troubling illness, with my absence from the kind of Church service I have been appointed to give—including executive function—has been assuaged greatly by the realization of a personal ministry to lift, guide, love, and bless. The Lord has simply put me in the path of many individuals who need to find a greater sense of peace in their own lives, and I have had the opportunity to "minister grace." I would not claim to any success in this personal ministry, what I do know is that such experiences have helped me to feel useful once again. I have gained a new sense of peace about my own role, my own situation, my own purpose, and my future.

I know that when we extend lines of hopeful credit to those whose life accounts seem empty, our own coffers of consolation are enriched and made full; our cup truly "runneth over" (Psalm 23:5).

President Spencer W. Kimball said, "A person cannot give a crust to the Lord without receiving a loaf in return" and, "Can you call it a sacrifice if you give up a handful of dust in return for a whole earth?"[91]

When we live to serve, serene peace will lift us.

Embrace Modesty

Wherever the word "modesty" is used, the immediate thought is in relation to modesty of dress. However, in regard to peace I invoke the term to cover not only that but also some other aspects of life, specifically in relation to attitudes, expectations, and personal behavior.

One of the damaging disturbances of our peace is our expectation that the acquisition of more and more material goods will make us happier—the most up-to-date cell phone, the fastest game console or gadget, an ever bigger home. We get attached to material possessions and feel disturbed when we do not have enough of them; not necessarily because of their inherent value to us or their usefulness, but increasingly because of our status with others. We not only want to "keep up with the Joneses," but we feel a need to surpass others in a never satiated ascendancy of acquisition. Modesty in our wants and needs is critical to a feeling of peaceful ease, but it often goes unrealized because of our almost inescapable thirst for more.

A major reason for the economic collapse and wracking recessions in the countries of the world in recent years can simply be summarized as greed. Greed by the "Wall Street" giants of industry and banking and the financial sector in general;, greed amongst some employees and employee groups who have demanded ever increasing remuneration for less productivity and economic output; greed of homeowners and mort-gage lenders who created a mortgage bubble that all but decimated the housing market as the "good times" came to a rapid end with the huge loss of equity, homes, and peace, and the attendant consequences of collapse of confidence and destructive despair. It has all been a disaster, largely of our own making.

I personally had to face the consequences of such a crisis when I made a failed business investment some years ago, financed by a second mortgage on our home. The aim was to realize a substantial level of wealth, arising from the new technology "bubble," at a time when home prices were ascending like a rocket and interest rates were low. Of course, the housing market collapsed faster than a deflated balloon, the IT bubble burst, and there was huge financial loss, leaving us with a debt that stayed with us for over nine years. It was foolish, and it was greedy. As with many others, we discovered that at some stage, "the chickens do come home to roost." At that point my wife and I decided that we were unlikely to ever be rich, and that it did not matter a jot.

Interestingly, when I became a General Authority of the Church and we suddenly had to leave our home in England, not expecting ever to return to it, we were left in a quandary about what to do with our house, our furniture, and all of the other "stuff" we had accumulated over twenty-seven years of marriage. It had all seemed so important.

One of our children, with his family of five, moved into our home and stayed for five years; we gave all of our furniture to them, including Dianne's hard won and prized piano. We then put all of our other "stuff" out into our backyard and invited members of our ward to come for a farewell social. The only condition was that they had to take some of our possessions away with them. It was like a yard sale without the "sale" element. Altogether, it was not a sad experience. We had stored some of our most valued items, but we have really not missed the rest of it at all. It was, and is, a sobering reminder that what matters most in life has little to do with bricks and mortar, stocks and shares, or lands and gold.

Incurring debt in order to finance more and more things, to satisfy more wants rather than needs, is so fearfully foolish. So much peace is disturbed, so many marriages are troubled due to excessive levels of debt. In an address with sound advice for young men, President Gordon B. Hinckley taught, "Be modest in your wants. You do not need a big home with a big mortgage. . . . You can and should avoid overwhelming debt. There is nothing that will cause greater tension in marriage than grinding debt, which will make of you a slave to your creditors. You may have to borrow money to begin ownership of a home. But do not let it be so costly that it will occupy your thoughts day and night."[92]

President Heber J. Grant said, "If there is any one thing that will bring peace and contentment into the human heart, and into the family, it is to live within our means. And if there is one thing that is grinding and discouraging and disheartening, it is to have debts and obligations that one cannot meet."[93]

In the priesthood session of the October 1998 general conference, President Hinckley related how President James E. Faust had dealt with his debt. President Hinckley said, "President Faust would not tell you this himself . . . he had a mortgage on his house drawing four percent interest. Many people would have told him he was foolish to pay off that mortgage when it carried so low a rate of interest. But the first opportunity he had to acquire some means, he and his wife determined they would pay off their mortgage. He has been free of debt since that day. That's why he wears a smile on his face, and that's why he whistles while he works."[94]

Being modest in our wants and desires and staying out of debt is both wise and peaceful. The most elite car, the classiest furniture, the largest home, individually and collectively do not really matter. In the eternal scheme of things, their possession, or lack of possession, is of no consequence at all.

Possessions do not bring peace. That comes only in and through obedience to the commandments and is conveyed through the priceless comforting companionship of the Holy Ghost.

We can also be modest in our expressions and in our speech by limiting noise and irreverence, not giving in to loud, riotous laughter or enjoyment at the misfortunes of others, and avoiding ill speaking and extremity of views. Remember that we are to use words that "minister grace unto the hearers"; this encompasses ourselves and our families. Biting our tongue on occasions can contribute much to the peace of others, as well as to our own. Some take an element of pride in saying, "Well, you know me, I always speak my mind," as if that is some kind of virtue. There are times when we should keep our thoughts to ourselves and be economical in expression. There is much to be gained through modesty of speech. It is far from virtuous to destroy the good name and peace of others.

Living in modest surroundings can also increase a sense of peace. This includes keeping our homes clean and free of clutter. Whenever we enter a home that is quiet, neat, tidy, and clean there is an automatic sense of peace that descends; so should it be for our own homes. They do not need to be lavish, it is often quite the opposite. Modesty in our surroundings can be just as important as modesty in dress.

These are some of the lifestyle "peaceful pathways" that can make a great difference to our own sense of peaceful equilibrium. The reader may have others to add to this list. These concepts, and the other aspects of peace—including ways that are explored in this book—are the drivers of attaining peace in our lives. It can be done.

CHAPTER 8

Peaceful Perspectives

*O*ur peace can be disturbed if we do not keep things in their proper perspective. This chapter explores some of the ways in which peace-promoting perspective can provide helpful context when dealing with issues that drain our sense of peace.

Sufficient unto the Day

Our peace is often disturbed by our worrying unduly about things that actually do not matter very much, or worrying over something that may occur in the future, but which has not yet happened. Instead of taking care of the present, we spend our emotional and mental reserves on something that may never happen at all. There is a well-known saying, "Take care of today and tomorrow will take care of itself." Its origin, of course, comes from one of the Savior's teachings from the Sermon on the Mount, the greatest sermon that was ever preached: "Take therefore no thought for the morrow: for the morrow shall take thought for the things of itself. Sufficient unto the day is the evil thereof" (Matthew 6:34).

Some may choose to interpret this as meaning: do what you like today without regard of the consequences; what it leads to, or "the morrow," does not matter very much and should not be worried about today. This is foolish. We do have to be wise in the decisions we make and the actions we take today. Besides, this teaching of the Savior comes immediately after the instructions, "take no thought, saying, what shall we eat? or, What shall we drink? or, Wherewithal shall we be clothed? (For after all these things do the Gentiles seek:) for your Heavenly Father knoweth that ye have need of all these things. But seek ye first the kingdom of God, and his righteousness; and all these things shall be added unto you" (Matthew 6:31–33).

In other words, do not seek the things of the world, but be engaged in building up the kingdom of God, then good will follow. I firmly believe that putting God first in reality means that we have put ourselves first. Put God first, and everything else falls into place. After all, we will always be in His debt, not the other way around. In this context, taking "no thought for the morrow" does not mean having a laissez-faire attitude to the future, but doing what needs to be done, fixing what needs to be fixed today. Why worry about things that might never happen or things that are of little consequence even if they do? That is a recipe for a lifetime of total worry and stress. We may as well lock ourselves in a cupboard. It is so futile, so stultifying. It is frankly foolish and even ridiculous, verging on mania.

Unnecessary worry leads to total inaction and a day full of discontent. If we are not careful we can become addicted to anxiety instead of being filled with fearless faith, filled with earthly excruciation rather than eternal elation. Torturing ourselves today is self-defeating and dreadfully debilitating. We cannot be at peace if we are constantly worrying about the future—sufficient unto the day.

Change What Needs to Be Changed

In what has become known as "The Serenity Prayer," Reinhold Niebuhr wrote:

> God, give me grace to accept with serenity
> The things that cannot be changed,
> Courage to change the things
> Which should be changed,
> And the wisdom to distinguish
> The one from the other.
>
> Living one day at a time,
> Enjoying one moment at a time,
> Accepting hardship as a pathway to peace,
> Taking, as Jesus did,

This sinful world as it is,
Not as I would have it.
Trusting that You will make all things right,
If I surrender to Your will,
So that I may be reasonably happy in this life,
And supremely happy with You forever in the next."[95]

The message is if there are things that are not right today that you can change today, then change them. If there are things that are not right today but which you cannot change today, stop fretting about them.

President Harold B. Lee said, "The most important of all the commandments of God is that one that you are having the most difficulty keeping today. If it is one of dishonesty, if it is one of unchastity, if it is one of falsifying, not telling the truth, today is the day for you to work on that until you have been able to conquer that weakness. Put that aright and then you start on the next one that is most difficult for you to keep. That's the way to sanctify yourself by keeping the commandments of God."[96]

It is quite simple really: if we are doing something that we should not be doing, stop it! If we are not doing something that we should be doing, start it!

Derek A. Cuthbert, my mission president, often taught: "Now is the time! This is the day! We are the people!"[97]

Taking charge of today and making any changes that we need and can change is what will bring peaceful happiness.

Keep the Faith

A significant way to obtain peace is to do what we should be doing. It is no surprise that Heavenly Father's eternal plan is also referred to as the plan of happiness. Even in the midst of trial and opposition we can obtain peace if we do what we should be doing.

As highlighted earlier, in approximately 40 BC, the humble followers of Christ in America were wading through their affliction. We read, "Nevertheless they did fast and pray oft, and did wax stronger and stronger in their humility, and firmer and firmer in the faith in Christ, unto the filling their souls with joy and consolation, yea, even to the purifying and the sanctification of their hearts, which sanctification cometh because of their yielding their hearts unto God" (Helaman 3:35).

Could there be some who are losing consolation because faith, fasting, prayer, and submission to the will of the Father have been put to one side while discontent, pride, and fear have been allowed to run riot with their emotions?

To think good thoughts, do good things. Act in faith. Keep the faith.

Be Happy

There is so much to be happy about as we step out to enjoy what is all around us. I was in Philadelphia on business when terrorists struck New York's Twin Towers. Another plane had crash-landed in Pennsylvania, so it was not all that far away.

Like many others, I watched on TV all of the ghastly events unfold. We were all in a state of deep shock.

Then I went out to walk around the city and felt a sense of peace and hope that was almost tangible. I was struck by how the usual busyness had come to a stop. Everything was a little slower, more peaceful, and less manic. Street noise diminished; soothing, sacred music filtered through church doors; there seemed to be greater courtesy and less jarring hurly-burly.

My initial thought was everyone was simply in a state of shock, no doubt many were, but then I felt something else, a quiet resolve to simply rise above it all.

It would not be true to say that people became happy; we know they did not. There were examples of grief everywhere, but there was something else—the emergence of a deep resolve to put things right, to restore America's equilibrium, and to find peace again. Within hours, the Stars and Stripes adorned every vehicle and the windows of the now respectfully closed stores and salons. It was peace, not hysteria that enveloped the city, peace and a desire to serve and to help. I saw evidence of the quiet, peaceful pride that makes America great.

Of course, in the midst of the devastation in downtown New York, there was a great rush, a great commotion as emergency services rushed from one scene to the other. Building dust covered the people, bodies were removed, and families frantically sought for loved ones, all on top of anxiety of the possibility of further attack. However, in the end of it all, it was not fear that prevailed, it was acceptance, love, hope, and peace. While many families are still totally traumatized, the general population has managed to restore a level of equilibrium and have got on with life, reminded of vulnerability, and almost humbled.

I had been due to return to Britain the following day, but flight disruption made that impossible, so I was forced to remain in Philadelphia for almost one week. It was a peaceful week as I sat in parks watching the people going about their business, tourists still happily lining up to give dignified homage to the Liberty Bell and Independence Hall.

As I walked through parks, birds were still chirping, flowers were still gloriously blooming, children were playing, concerned but loving mothers were looking on, ice cream was being sold, and some entertainment was playing in various places.

An older man sat down unsteadily next to me on a bench. He refused help to descend or rise, determined to do it all himself. We spoke for some time and I discovered he was an eighty-four-year-old widower named Manny, a German Jew who had suffered through all of the atrocities of the Nazi devastation. He chirpily talked of the new "love of his life," also a widow. She was, he said, "a sprightly young seventy-five." They were engaged to be married and were meeting for lunch. Then, with a twinkle in his eye, he moved off to hide behind a tree to surprise her as she walked along. I secretly prayed that her heart was strong enough to withstand the shock. He brought his sweetheart over to see me, we had a pleasant chat, and they invited me to join them for lunch. I was tempted to do so, but decided not to get in the way of the lovebirds, and made my excuses. We exchanged contact information and stayed in touch for a while. Manny died and not so long after, letters from his sweetheart wife also stopped. I assume that she had gone to join him.

As I reflected on that experience, I wondered at how, in the midst of chaos and turmoil just eighty or so miles away, I had witnessed something that was touchingly tender, a late spring. It felt whole, good, and peaceful. I went back to my hotel room, a somewhat more peaceful and content man. I had found peace amid calamity.

I am convinced that we can each find things to be happy about, even if our current circumstances are less than enviable. We are each writing our own book, and we should not allow some unhappy passages to bring dismay to the chapters yet to be written. As long as we are breathing, the book is still a work in progress. Find happy things, make them happier, enjoy them, and write them down. Your own record of happy experiences can be read over and over again; they will bring you peace.

In the aftermath of my brain tumor problems, I experienced a seizure while speaking at a stake conference. I felt embarrassed and devastated; it had been one of my worst fears. However, I was blessed by the Lord and the seizure was not major. I recovered quickly and was able to start again from exactly where I had left off. I had not "skipped a beat." I had even been in the midst of quoting the scripture from the dedicatory prayer of the Kirtland Temple in which the Lord promised that in the midst of world calamities, his people would "not faint in the day of trouble" (Doctrine & Covenants 109:38).

A ripple of laughter had already begun before I was able to say, "Well I did not faint, at least." I was blessed to carry on to the end of the meeting, although I was so weary and unsteady afterward that I had to leave the stand as soon as the meeting was over, forgoing my customary shaking of hands.

As I wondered later why it had all happened, I felt a miracle had occurred in front of some two thousand people. The miracle was not that this had been prevented in the first place. The miracle of seizure removal did not happen, because it was not meant to happen.

It having occurred, however, brought the real miracle of my ability to carry on. I felt that other miracles would have begun to unfold in the lives of the congregation. For a start, they paid much more attention to the remainder of the talk! More seriously though, I reflected that there were likely some there who had their own physical, emotional, or spiritual burdens to carry. My hope is that they will first have seen that others, even the Lord's servants, suffer similar ailments and that we can bounce back, and still do good things despite it all. Perhaps that was the real miracle that day. I have come to terms and am at peace with it all.

We may sometimes wish that things could be different, but we can also find happiness and joy in what we have and in the blessings that are already ours. Contentment brings peace, so be content.

Self-deprecating humor can also bring a wave of peace. While writing this book, away from my home and my office, I often needed to have a document exchange with my secretary. She would pass on the completed work to the publisher, and I would pass new chapters to her. Then, because of the good offer of a friend, we were able to spend a few weeks in Park City for convalescence while I was undergoing further chemotherapy treatment. I, therefore, had to send chapters by mail to my office. Worried that they may get lost in the post, we went off to a local copy shop, had a copy made, and then placed the work in an envelope, and into the mail. The only thing is that I posted the copy as well as the original, making the copying a complete waste of time and causing the same concern I was trying to solve.

How foolish can one person be? I felt less than happy, totally ridiculous, really, until I got to the point of realization that there was nothing now to be done other than hope it arrived. It also helped that Dianne and I just felt it was so funny, ludicrous really, so we laughed about it for most of the day. We can be happy even in the midst of unhappy things. Perhaps we may even need to laugh at ourselves from time to time.

Eternal Focus

Not all things have eternal significance. In our work, our lives, and our service it is well to focus on the ends themselves and not just the means to get to that end. For example, in the Church we have a mandated desire to "watch over each member." That is the goal, the end. Even further, the reason we are directed to "watch over every member" is also a way toward one ultimate "end" that is to help each other attain celestial glory.

One of the means of attaining that end is through home and visiting teaching. They are not the goal, they are one of the means to the goal. Sadly, one could easily be forgiven for thinking otherwise when observing what happens in meetings and phone calls. If I had a dollar for every time I have heard something to the effect of, "Brethren, we only have one week left to get our home teaching done," I would be a rich man. The aim is to help others achieve their eternal exaltation, not to "get our home teaching done."

It is not about reports or the number of visits that are made. Home and visiting teaching are simply current programs that help us to focus on reaching out, helping, rescuing, lifting, and encouraging others on their gospel journeys, specifically in the making and keeping of gospel covenants and the obtaining of essential ordinances. While some ways of measurement can assist in fulfilling those responsibilities, the number of visits made does not fully reflect how such aid and watch care is being fulfilled. Home and visiting teaching have eternal significance, but our individual exaltation is not dependent on achieving one hundred percent activity in these programs. We must be careful not to get confused. Furthermore, we would do well to avoid getting caught up in what could best be described as "busy work," things that do not make much of a real difference to anyone. In this regard, I am reminded of a humorous song from the 1949 film, *A Connecticut Yankee in King Arthur's Court*, which was based on the 1889 Mark Twain novel of the same name. Bing Crosby sang the lyrics:

> We're busy doin' nothin'
> Workin' the whole day through
> Tryin' to find lots of things not to do
> We're busy goin' nowhere
> Isn't it just a crime
> We'd like to be unhappy, but
> We never do have the time."

Another verse continued in the same vein:

> I have to wake the Sun up
> He's liable to sleep all day
> And then inspect the rainbows
> So they'll be bright and gay
> I must rehearse the songbirds
> To see that they sing in key
> Hustle, bustle
> And never a moment free.

Endless meetings in which we talk about problem after problem, but never resolve what to do, or that fail to stimulate action, are meetings that are not worth having.

Some years ago, in a leadership training meeting that was running slightly late, the final speaker, President James E. Faust of the First Presidency, came to the pulpit and said, "A talk does not have to be endless to be eternal; in the name of Jesus Christ, Amen," and then he sat down. I doubt that I was the only one who was surprised, but it was a powerful lesson. I think he meant that we do not have to use a multiplicity of words to say something meaningful. I feel that in our own church service we can sometimes feel pressed to fill silence with rambling talk. I recall hearing a powerful testimony in a ward testimony meeting, from a young woman who simply stood up and said, "I know that obedience to the commandments is important; in the name of Jesus Christ, Amen." Then she sat down, having delivered a testimony of a principle in a single sentence and in a matter of seconds. It was rather stunning to a congregation that often had to sit through long speeches that were short in testimony.

Years ago, during my service as a stake president, there was a prompting to call a good man who had not been to any Church meeting for many years, to serve in a significant assignment, I issued the call and asked him how long it would take for him to be ready to serve. He looked down at the floor, and there was a long, long, period of interminable silence; it seemed to be going on for an eternity. I did something really important, I kept my mouth shut and did not say another word. I knew that during the physical silence in the room, the Holy Ghost was speaking to him, and this good brother was making inner resolutions. He finally looked up and said, "I will be ready in two weeks; I knew something was going to happen to change my life." Habits he had formed that went against the covenants he had made when he received the Melchizedek Priesthood were quickly discarded, as he suddenly began to see the things of greatest import in his life.

I recall an occasion when I heard President Faust counsel us to distinguish between needs and wants. As we keep our focus on eternal things, we will have neither time or inclination for the trivial, the distractions of the world.

While on an assignment to preside at a district conference in the Cook Islands, I visited with a brother who had stopped coming to Church not long after his baptism some fifteen months before. He greeted me with a cigarette between his fingers. During our discussion, he spoke lovingly of his three young daughters referring to them as his little angels. We then spoke about the opportunity he would have to take his angels, including his wife to the temple to be sealed together in an eternal family relationship, and I called him to get to the point where he could receive the Melchizedek Priesthood and a temple recommend. I asked if there was anything that would prevent that from happening, and he held up his cigarette. I then asked what would be more valuable to him, how he would rate, the use of tobacco or the blessing of an eternal family unit: "are you really going to sacrifice something that is way up high, your angels becoming yours forever, for something that is way down low, your smoking habit?" He reflected that the prospect of an eternal family was much more important than continuing to smoke. Our district conference the next day found him sitting on the front pew of the chapel, alongside his wife, their three little angels, and other relatives he had brought along.

Having an eternal focus also helps us to rise above peace-draining anxiety caused by reflecting on what we do not have.

Elder Dallin H. Oaks of the Quorum of the Twelve has confirmed, "We must learn to focus on things which are ends in themselves."[98]

The ultimate end, the whole purpose of our sojourn on earth, is to return to the presence of God with those we love at our side. That is what it means when we speak of fulfilling the measure of our creation; it is why we are here. If we lose that, we lose it all.

Labor for Life

Whilst there are times when we are each in need of periods of rest and relaxation, being bone-idle is not conducive to peace; it is quite the opposite in fact.

The Lord commanded, "Cease to be idle" (Doctrine & Covenants 88:124). Elder George Q. Cannon commented, "The spirit of the gospel of the Lord Jesus Christ is opposed to idleness. We do not believe that a man who has the spirit can rest content if he is not busily employed."[99]

We cannot be content and at peace if we are not productive and constructive. President Spencer W. Kimball taught, "The dignity and self-esteem that honest work produces are essential to happiness. It is so easy for leisure to turn into laziness."[100]

In sterling counsel, Elder George Q. Cannon stated, "Labor, instead of a curse has been a blessing to mankind. No bread is so sweet as that earned by honest toil. Labor is happiness; no heart is more joyful than the one busy with the works of love and duty. Labor is health; none are more vigorous than the laborer. Labor is life; without it we should stagnate."[101]

President Joseph F. Smith counseled:

> There should be no idlers in Zion. Even the poor who have to be assisted should be willing to do all in their power to earn their own living. Not one man or woman should be content to sit down and be fed, clothed, or housed without any exertion on his or her part to compensate for these privileges. All men and women should feel a degree of independence of character that would stimulate them to

do something for a living, and not be idle . . . it is necessary that we should be industrious, that we should intelligently apply our labor to something that is productive and conducive to the welfare of the human family.[102]

I like these words from Amelia Earhart, "Courage is the price that Life exacts for granting peace, the soul that knows it not, knows no release from little things." And, "The more one does and sees and feels, the more one is able to do, and the more genuine may be one's appreciation of fundamental things like home, and love, and understanding companionship."[103]

It is especially important that our young people, particularly young men, grow up with a smoldering passion to rely on their own work for the means of life that they need, to be self-reliant, to gain their bread from the sweat of their brow.

Of course, we live in an age in which economic downturn and recidivist recessions cause havoc, not just in money markets, but in homes and families, people and peace. Businesses fail—I know, I worked for one—and employment is lost. Unemployment is insidiously intrusive on personal peace. It is corrosive: it gnaws away at self-worth and a sense of personal usefulness. For this reason, unemployment has to be fought against and labor re-enthroned.

Of course, there are many who have immediate welfare needs that they cannot meet through personal efforts. Assistance, such as Church welfare support, may be needed for a season. Even then, we do not help another by simply providing support without including some opportunity for work. In Scotland, our mission home was a substantial house set in splendid and expansive grounds. Many vagrants would call at the back door seeking support. Sister Cuthbert, the magnificent wife of our mission president, always wanted to help, but not hinder. She believed in work, not dole. So, everyone was helped with some food, but they were also asked to do some work on the grounds.

We have to be careful that a necessary safety net does not become a welfare web. The need is for a ladder out of poverty, not a trapdoor that keeps someone below their self-satisfying potential.

The first thing that someone who has lost a full-time job can do is to work full time to find a full-time job, any job. Expectations of level and type of work may need to be set to one side in favor of just getting a job. Any job is better than no job. Those who have been at the top may need to be humble enough to accept an entry-level position. Even though menial work may seem humbling for an unemployed executive, it may be all that can be obtained and will enable entry back into the workplace. The wage may be a million miles away from previous perks and salaries, but it is at least a wage, an income that is earned rather than money that is given. I know a young husband who could find no other work than cleaning public toilets, so that is what he did. Of course, the pay was abysmal, and the work as menial as it possibly could be. However, he persevered. He just could not do otherwise. He was able to provide for his family, and he gained the blessings that flow from honest labor. He now runs a successful business and also serves in a significant way in the Church.

President Heber J. Grant stated, "I assert with confidence that the law of success, here and hereafter, is to have a humble and a prayerful heart, and to work, work, work."[104]

Whatever it takes, work is better than idleness. Honest work leads to contentment, fulfillment, happiness, and peace.

CHAPTER 9

Peace at Home

The first and foremost place in which to create conditions of peaceful existence is within the walls of our own home. In fact, if we do not feel at peace at home, it is hard to feel at peace anywhere. This chapter explores various aspects of peace at home—ways in which feelings of peace can be nurtured and experienced by all.

Children Are "an Heritage"

Children are sometimes seen as "possessions"—they are not. Men and women are allowed the great privilege to bear and care for children. It is a sacred trust, and there is no greater influence we can have on the future of the world than to raise children in truth and light, in tenderness and love.

The Psalmist declared, "Lo, children are an heritage of the Lord" (Psalm 127:3). This is a pertinent reminder that our children are the Lord's, first and last, and it is our sacred privilege to care for them and aid them during their sojourn through mortality. They, like us, were with Heavenly Father before they came to earth, and it is our mission to take them home to Him.

President Spencer W. Kimball taught, "We do not rear children just to please our vanity. We bring children into the world to become kings and queens, and priests and priestesses for our Lord."[105]

The Lord's expectations are set out by President David O. McKay, "Next to eternal life, the most precious gift that our Father in Heaven can bestow upon man is his children."[106] Further, "There are three fundamental things to which every child is entitled. First, a respected name; second, a sense of security; third, opportunities for development."[107]

My emphasis on the heritage and place of children in our lives is because we have the absolute duty to help them have a secure foundation of peace in their own life. It is very hard for children who have not experienced love, respect, and peace at home to later feel and cultivate such feelings in their own lives and in their own homes.

When our first child, David, was born, I was filled with a sense of awe. I held him in my arms and felt this sacred trust from Heavenly Father. I whispered in his little ear how much I already loved him, how privileged I felt to be the father to whom the Lord had entrusted him. I made him promises of how I would care for and help him throughout his life, that I would lead him home to eternal life. Throughout his life I have tried to be true to those promises. On the day of his sealing in the London England Temple, when I put my arms around him, the memory of that occasion came flooding back as if it had happened just the day before. It was an intimately personal, sweet, and spiritual experience; no wonder I wept.

One of the rather detrimental and somewhat despicable aspects of our modern world is the way in which children have become commodities. In our age of celebrity it almost seems that children have become something of an accessory. One wonders what the future holds for such children brought up in a world of celebrity, sometimes in homes where stability and decency are more notable for their absence than presence; and where the acquisition of a child seems to be used as a means of bringing some kind of validation to a particular lifestyle of those who become "parents." These experiments with children and the new definitions of family are like playing Russian roulette with the future.

Within Heavenly Father's plan for the happiness and salvation of His children, the little ones who come to earth are heavenly gifts. They are "entitled to birth within the bonds of matrimony, and to be reared by a father and mother who honor marital vows with complete fidelity."[108]

On one occasion, when one of our small children was being particularly fractious and annoying, I expressed frustration. In Dianne's gentle way she said, "Oh, David, she will only be here with us for such a little while." It was a valuable lesson for me.

We do well to remember how precious each of these little ones are to the Lord—even when they are in their interesting teenage years—and our responsibility to love, care, nurture, provide, and protect. We can, and should, help them to feel security and peace.

Absence of Anger

Our homes can only be places of peace if there is an absence of anger between husbands and wives, parents and children. Parents set the tone for all that happens in the home. Not only that, how a child behaves outside of the home is often a reflection of what he or she has experienced within the home.

If voices are raised in anger, if there is tumult, annoyance, fury, and drama, there will be no peace at home or in the lives of family members. If parents argue and disagree, curse and swear, yell and are violent, it should not be surprising when we see a child following suit. It is all woefully withering for them and their parents, communities, and future generations.

A father's role is to bring peace rather than engender fear; to embrace a child with love and uplift rather than inflict physical pain.

Some of the specific behaviors that should simply be in evidence in our homes are

- Parents who show respect for each other—no violent arguments, derisory comments, or raised voices.

- Individual goodness: both parents demonstrating faith, gospel maturity, and decent behavior.

- Parental harmony, with each investing 100 percent into their union. Some couples say they have a "50-50" marriage. Why? Can they not each give 100 percent of their time, devotion, and energy to each other, to problem solving, to their family, and to their children? Marriage and parenting is not about division of responsibility, it is about the sharing of a sacred trust in which each spouse gives all of themselves. To do less is a dereliction of marital and parental responsibility.

- Respect between spouses and with children, using words that build and strengthen, rather than demean and destroy.

- Parents who emphasize and demonstrate virtue.

- Total absence of physical violence.

This last issue, of avoiding abrogation of agency, is fundamental to true happiness and peace. Seeking to control others, in effect removing their agency, is unrighteous dominion, plain and simple. Impatience, intolerance, and imposition of will are satanic. In response to Heavenly Father's plan, Lucifer said that he would make sure everyone would obey. "Surely, I will do it" (Moses 4:1). He was cast down and rejected, not just because he wanted all of the glory for himself, but also because he "sought to destroy the agency of man, which I, the Lord God, had given him" (Moses 4:3).

It can be tempting to abrogate the agency of members of our family. It is not peace-inducing. If parents always "lay down the law," especially to teenagers, peace cannot prevail. Our teenagers need to know that while we may trust them, we do not trust "the world"; we do not trust Satan. If one spouse seeks to totally control the other, with destructive drama if their will is not followed, there can be no peace.

President David O. McKay taught,

> I can imagine few if any things more objectionable in the home than the absence of unity and harmony. On the other hand, I know that a home in which unity, mutual helpfulness, and love abide is just a bit of heaven on earth. . . .
>
> I cherish the remembrance that never once as a lad in the home of my youth did I ever see one instance of discord between father and mother, and that goodwill and mutual understanding have been the uniting bond that has held together a fortunate group of brothers and sisters. Unity, harmony, goodwill are virtues to be fostered and cherished in every home.[109]

On another occasion, President McKay taught, "No member of this Church—husband, father, or child—has the right to utter an oath in his home or even to express a cross word to his wife or to his children or to parents. We contribute to an ideal home by our character, by controlling our passions, our temper, by guarding our speech, because those things will make our homes what they are."[110]

Many of these principles were spoken of in a landmark address by President Gordon B. Hinckley,

Now, I believe that most marriages in the Church are happy, that both husbands and wives in these marriages experience a sense of security and love, of mutual dependence, and an equal sharing of burdens. I am confident that the children in these homes, at least in the vast majority of them, are growing up with a sense of peace and security, knowing that they are appreciated and loved by both of their parents, who, they feel, love one another. But I am confident, my brethren, that there is enough of the opposite to justify what I am saying.[111]

He read a portion of a letter he had received from an unhappy wife who had written of her husband who, despite his virtues, had a "strong streak of authoritarianism. . . . his volatile temper flares up often enough to remind me of all the ugliness of which he is capable."[112]

President Hinckley went on to say, "Who can calculate the wounds inflicted, their depth and pain, by harsh and mean words spoken in anger? . . . A violent temper is such a terrible, corrosive thing. And the tragedy is that it accomplishes no good; it only feeds evil with resentment and rebellion and pain."[113]

When I was a very young boy, during my mother's second marriage, I was so frightfully scared all of the time that I slept with a hammer under my pillow. Looking back, I do not know what I ever thought I would do with it. However, it helped to replace at least some element of fear with a modicum of security. I cannot say that it brought peace, but it did bring a feeling of safety. Peace only came when that marriage ended, and the man I feared had gone never to return. I was glad to be able to put the hammer away; not only because a feeling of peace had come to me, but also because it had not been all that comfortable.

Parents, especially fathers, have a great responsibility to inculcate peace in their own homes.

Wisdom in All Things

Peace at home can also be disturbed by excessive noise and over-burdened schedules. Quietness in our world has been replaced by noise, such as from raucous entertainment and the shrill, high-decibel antics of those who participate in so-called reality shows that fill our television screens every day. Fast moving electronic games destroy quietness, some of these portraying war scenes of violence, viciousness, gore, and graphic terror. We have to be vigilant and wise.

More than ever before, parents have been largely reduced to manic taxi drivers on evenings and weekends, rushing their children from one event to the next: dance, football, soccer, basketball, karate, tournaments of one kind or another. Children are caught up, often with parental urging, in a never-ending round of competitions and permanent activity with little opportunity to just "be still." At times there is no letup; no time to breathe; no time to simply rest, relax, and be at peace. Somehow, there needs to be balance between talent, development, and opportunities to relax. Can we not be wise?

The Church environment can also become too busy. President Spencer W. Kimball wisely counseled, "As local Church leaders cautiously conserve the time that families can spend together, we say to both parents and children, 'Come back home.' Parents should spend less time in clubs, bowling alleys, banquets, and social gatherings, and more time with their children. Young men and women must balance their involvement in school and other social activities with supportive participation in family activities and appropriate time in the home."[114]

The consolidated meeting schedule was introduced when I was a young bishop. It removed the necessity of mid-week Relief Society and Primary meetings, and reduced Sunday services from two to one, including shortening the time for sacrament meeting from ninety minutes to seventy minutes. One of the reasons for the change was to allow more time for families to be at home, and leaders were instructed to respect that time. It is sad when that direction is forgotten.

We now have a barrage of activities and events—multiple camps, various youth conferences, an array of sports events, hikes, golf tournaments, festivals, treks, and the like. While each may have a good purpose and can be individually justified, the amalgam of them all has eroded much time at home.

There are even additional events around stake conferences that may add to the burden of families at a time when parents are busy. For example, if the stake presidency feels that an invitation for members to attend a session of the temple before a stake conference is desirable, it would be wise to consider carefully how this can be done so that the time requirement on families is minimized.

Even in our Sunday meetings we can have too many people rushing around with bulging briefcases, clipboards, and sign-up sheets, instead of sitting with open scriptures and time for quiet reflection and peace.

We should be able to go home from Church with strengthened faith and peace, not with an even greater list of things we have to do. There is no divine law that says every class has to conclude with a teacher giving class members three or four things to do. Certainly, no speaker in sacrament meeting should give assignments to the congregation. Of course, we know that "faith, if it hath not works, is dead, being alone" (James 2:17), but let us also observe that works without faith are equally sterile.

In a sterling talk titled "O, Be Wise," Elder M. Russell Ballard, of the Quorum of the Twelve Apostles, observed,

> Occasionally we find some who become so energetic in their Church service that their lives become unbalanced. They start believing that the programs they administer are more important than the people they serve. They complicate their service with needless frills and embellishments that occupy too much time, cost too much money. . . . As a result of their focusing too much time and energy on their Church service, eternal and family relationships can deteriorate. . . . This is not healthy, spiritually or otherwise. . . . We need to strive to keep things in proper balance. We should never allow our service to replace the attention needed by other important priorities in our lives."[115]

Elder Ballard then set out six principles in which we could serve wisely and well:

1. Focus on people, not programs
2. Be innovative
3. Delegate responsibility
4. Eliminate guilt
5. Thoughtfully allocate resources
6. Extend appropriate responsibilities

It is worth considering further the penultimate paragraph of Elder Ballard's talk: "Brothers and sisters, be wise with your families. Be wise in fulfilling your Church callings. Be wise with your time. Be wise in balancing all of your responsibilities. O be wise, my beloved brothers and sisters. What can I say more?"

We would also do well to avoid leaders stepping in too fast to provide solutions to perceived problems in the homes and lives of our members, or get in the way of the revelation to which they are entitled. Unless specific help is requested by individuals and families, they should be left alone. President Boyd K. Packer, President of the Quorum of the Twelve Apostles, referred to what he described as an "epidemic of counselitis,"

> [which] drains spiritual strength from the Church, much like the common cold drains more out of humanity than any other disease. . . .
>
> If we lose our emotional and spiritual independence, our self-reliance, we can be weakened quite as much, perhaps even more, than when we become dependent materially. If we are not careful, we can lose the power of individual revelation.
>
> Spiritual independence and self-reliance is a sustaining power in the Church. If we rob the members of that, how can they get revelation for themselves? How will they know there is a prophet of God? How can they get answers to prayers? How can they know for *sure* for themselves?[116]

If we are wise, families will not be overburdened with programs or with interventions that prevent their own receipt of revelation. As such revelation flows, and as families have time to strengthen relationships in their own homes, lives will be filled with peace.

Praiseworthy Praise

I have heard it said that we should be "stinting in criticism, and lavish with praise." I generally subscribe to that sentiment, as long as we are honest in the praise and it is worthy of accolade. I feel that we can unhappily damage the future peace of our children if we overdo praise for even the smallest thing. Not everything is a "good job" or "awesome"—a word that is greatly misused in modern parlance.

We devalue the currency of language when we use words that do not really match the action. Whilst we should give words of encouragement, they should be appropriate, measured, and true. After all, not every child who stumbles through a "plinky-plonky" piano piece will be a concert pianist; but they could become a ward organist.

Our children cannot be the "best" at everything, or even "one of the best." Some parents seem anxious to extol to others every achievement of their children, to present a "perfect picture" of their family—perhaps as validation of their own role as parents—and then become very disturbed when that image is dented in some way. It has been interesting to note that, often, when I inquire about a couple's children,

I hear something to the effect of "they have all done wonderfully well, John is a senior banker, Mary is a world-class neurosurgeon, James is a leading lawyer." I cannot recall anyone ever saying something to the effect of, "John is a superb husband and loving father, Mary is a real disciple of Jesus Christ, James has great faith and spiritual maturity."

The question arises as to what we consider important, and if we are preparing our children for a world in which they will not always be "the best" at everything. Without a strong foundation and grasp of the difference between "how things are," and "how things can be," we close off desire for further development and increase the chance of discontent and lack of peace as the realities of life engulf them. Development of faith, testimony, and spiritual strength are vastly more important than playing in a school band or weekly participation in a ballet class.

We can be honest with our children and others without being unkind. L. Z. Granderson, a CNN contributor, related this experience:

> When my son was in middle school, I remember attending one of his school band concerts that wasn't very good.
>
> In fact, it sucked.
>
> At times it sounded as if half the band was playing one song and the other half was playing something totally different. And because I don't want my son to grow up a loser, I told him straight out what I thought.
>
> "How was it?" He asked. "It was pretty bad," I said. "I know, right?" My son agreed, smiling. "We're not good at all." And then we both laughed until we had tears in our eyes.[117]

I have long admired the wisdom and prescience set out in the poem "If", written in 1895 by Britain's Poet Laureate and Nobel Prize Winner, Rudyard Kipling.

> If you can keep your head when all about you
> Are losing theirs and blaming it on you,
> If you can trust yourself when all men doubt you,
> But make allowance for your doubting too;
> If you can wait and not be tired of waiting,
> Or being lied about, don't deal in lies,
> Or being hated, don't give way to hating,
> And yet don't look good, nor talk too wise;

If you can dream—and not make dreams your master;
If you can think—and not make thoughts your aim,
If you can meet with Triumph and Disaster
And treat those two imposters just the same;
If you can bear to hear the truth you've spoken
Twisted by knaves to make a trap for fools,
Or watch the things you gave your life to, broken,
And stoop and build'em up with worn-out tools;

If you can make one heap of all your winning:
And risk it all on one turn of pitch-and-toss,
And lose, and start again at your beginnings
And never breathe a word about your loss;
If you can force your heart and nerve and sinew
To serve your turn long after they are gone,
And so hold on when there is nothing in you
Except the Will which says to them: "Hold On!"

If you can talk with crowds and keep your virtue,
Or walk with kings—nor lose the common touch,
If neither foes nor loving friends can hurt you,
If all men count with you, but none too much;
If you can fill the unforgiving minute
With sixty seconds worth of distance run,
Yours is the Earth, and everything that's in it,
And—which is more—you'll be a Man, my son![118]

Peace begins at home. We would do well to promote aspiration, tempered by wisdom and understanding that not all of our dreams are fulfilled, not all of our ambitions are realized, and that some things are more important than others. There is no easy answer as to how this balance can be struck; most parents want to promote a sense of achievement and the sentiment that we can each rise to great heights, at the same time as helping children avoid the dangers of building houses of straw. I have met many who are desolate because of unfulfilled ambitions that were frankly not very realistic in the first place. Only a father and mother, working together in harmony and love, can determine how this should be approached. Part of it could be open discussion with our children on what they think it would take to achieve a particular goal or ambition; in other words, the price that has to be paid, and if they are willing to pay that price, as well as what they would have as a back-up plan if what they set their hearts on is not achieved. It would be good, however, if there could be in the midst of all else, the promotion of the understanding that our individual peace depends on who we have become even more than what we have done, that it is more about who we are than what we do.; that our true source of peace rests with the Prince of Peace, with the approbation of heaven, not with the applause of the world.

CHAPTER 10

The Prince of Peace

*W*e regularly speak and testify of Jesus Christ as the Messiah, the Redeemer, the Atoning One, the Divine Son of our Heavenly Father, our Lord, and our King. Less often spoken or testified of is Jesus Christ's role as "The Prince of Peace" (Isaiah 9:6). This is not only a great pity, it is also a deprivation to us.

In gospel terms, the Savior is clearly preeminent as heir to the throne of God, and He provides for each of us as children of God an opportunity to be "heirs of God, and joint-heirs with Christ" (Romans 8:17).

In describing the Messiah as the "Prince of Peace," Isaiah recognized His preeminent position as the source and deliverer of peace to the world and to the human heart.

There are numerous and pervasive scriptural references to Jesus Christ as the source of peace. Paul describes the Savior as "he [who] is our peace" (Ephesians 2:14), and later blesses the Thessalonians, "Now the Lord of peace himself give you peace always by all means" (2 Thessalonians 3:16).

The Psalmist prophesied, "He will speak peace unto his people, and to his saints" (Psalm 85:8). Testifying in the court of King Noah, Abinadi referred to Christ as "the founder of peace" (Mosiah 15:8). Of course, the clearest declaration that Christ is the provider of peace fell from His own lips; as His final blessing to His chosen apostles, He said, "Peace I leave with you, my peace I give unto you: not as the world giveth, give I unto you. Let not your heart be troubled, neither let it be afraid" (John 14:27).

This blessing of peace, emanating as it does from the Savior, was not just for the original Twelve, it is also for each one of us. It is a blessing for you!

When we have received this peace ourselves, the Lord can then use us as His messengers or instruments of peace in blessing the lives of others. There are many all around us who are in need of love, care, understanding, and support. Some feel marginalized, some have been ostracized; many have challenges, disruption, lifestyles, attitudes, or behaviors that may cause them to feel somewhat distant from the Church. Some face dark feelings of loneliness, despair, lack of love, or a total lack of peace.

We can each do something about the angst, fear, and disturbance of others. We can help others feel the encompassing love and comfort that emanates from the Prince of Peace. Many feel a sense of peace when one of us simply says, "Jesus loves you. I love you. We accept you. How can I help you?" We can, and should, be peacemakers; not just in our own lives, in our own homes and communities, but also in the lives of others. We can help others feel a deep sense of peace just by what we say and do to help, uplift, and love.

The Lord needs us to act on His behalf by bringing feelings of love and peace to others; it is even our charge, our sacred commission. This royal heritage that emanates from the Prince of Peace is perhaps best described in the words of Peter:

"But ye are a chosen generation, a royal priesthood, an holy nation, a peculiar people; that ye should shew forth the praises of him who hath called out of darkness into his marvelous light." (1 Peter 2:9).

Having established our pedigree, Peter continues with counsel as to the implications for us in our own role as peacemakers:

"Having your conversation honest among the Gentiles: that whereas they speak against you as evildoers, they may by your good works, which they shall behold, glorify God in the day of visitation." (1 Peter 2:12) In royal terms, Jesus is the Prince of Peace and we are each a duke or a duchess with the same charge.

Of course, the Twelve would not have been surprised by the Savior's self-declaration identification of His being the source of peace. After all, they had seen with their own eyes the way in which Jesus had brought calm to boisterous waves, even walking on top of still waters.

In the midst of the Savior's second Galilean ministry, He came to Capernaum on the shores of Galilee. By then, as Matthew records, there were "great multitudes about him" (Matthew 8:18). Little wonder. The people had heard the magnificent Sermon on the Mount and parables such as that of a house built on rock or sand and the sower. They had witnessed that He "taught them as one having authority, and not as the scribes" (Matthew 7:29).

There had been miracles too: the restoration to life of the son of the widow of Nain, the healing of Peter's mother-in-law, and the healing of the centurion's servant. After Christ's all-embracing words of salvation, "I will come and heal him" (Matthew 8:7), there followed an entire evening in which "they brought unto him many that were possessed with devils: and he cast out the spirits with his word, and healed all that were sick" (Matthew 8:16).

Perhaps to obtain some respite from the multitudes, He "entered into a ship" (Matthew 8:23), described by Farrar as "His favourite pulpit"[119] to travel to the other side of the Sea of Galilee. It was during that journey that another mighty and famous miracle was to be observed by the apostles who were with Him.

"And there arose a great storm of wind, [Matthew calls it a tempest] and the waves beat into the ship, so that it was now full. And he was in the hinder part of the ship, asleep on a pillow: and they awake him, and say unto him, Master, carest thou not that we perish? And he arose, and rebuked the wind, and said unto the sea, Peace, be still. And the wind ceased, and there was a great calm" (Mark 4:37–39).

In the midst of the tempest of our lives, we can be brought to "great calm" as we too call upon the Master. If He has the power to cause the wind to cease and the waves to subside from the deck of a ship, He can, from the sanctuary of heaven, certainly still our distress and bring the chill winds of trouble in our lives to a stop. It is not just Galilee that can be made a place of peace; it is also possible in our minds, our hearts, and our very souls.

Such peace comes to those who have reposed their love, trust, loyalty, and faith in Jesus Christ, the Prince of Peace. We can pray for such faith, calling upon the Lord in our hours of need, and then trust Him, living as though our faith is already as deep as we hope it to become.

To the doubting Thomas, in words that must have been piercing, Jesus said, "Be not faithless, but believing" (John 20:27).

To those beside Him in the boat, no doubt still reeling from their terror and now somewhat stupefied by the miracle just witnessed, Jesus said, "Why are ye so fearful? How is it that ye have no faith? And they feared exceedingly, and said one to another, What manner of man is this, that even the winds and the sea obey him?" (Mark 4:40–41).

Indeed, what manner of man is this? A few years ago I found my wife in our bedroom crying gentle but deep tears. Having quickly established that I was not the cause, I inquired further. She had just been reading the account of the Savior's crucifixion, and wondered how, even at that awful moment of excruciating agony, vulnerability, and personal anguish, His only thoughts still seemed to be on how He could bless others. For those who had performed the crucifixion, and who were now parting His raiment in a disdainful act of gambling, He said, "Father, forgive them, for they know not what they do" (Luke 23:34), and to the thief on the cross by His side, "Today shalt thou be with me in paradise" (Luke 23:43).

Dianne told me that her tears flowed from two thoughts. What manner of man is this, who characteristically should think of others while suffering His own agonies? Then she said the other thought that caused her to weep further was the realization that as disciples we have to love as He loved, to treat others as He did, that this was the way to peace. She worried over her ability to do this, hence the tears.

Once the tempest had died and the winds ceased, the little band on the ship continued the journey to Bethsaida-Julias, a city built by Philip the Tetrarch. The Apostles had completed their first mission to preach and teach in their cities while Jesus had continued His ministry, clarifying doctrine such as that of fasting and what to do on the Sabbath day, as well as His ministry of healing, the raising of Jarius's daughter, the two blind men who were healed, and the casting out of evil spirits from the demoniac man.

When they reached Bethsaida-Julias, Jesus and the Apostles had spent time together in love, friendship, and fraternity. It was now the start of the third and final year of the Savior's mortal ministry.

Again, a huge crowd had gathered to hear Him and be blessed by Him. This was the place of the miraculous feeding of the five thousand from five barley loaves and two small fishes. The result among those who witnessed this was electrifying, saying, "This is of a truth that prophet that should come into the world" (John 6:14).

To avoid early acclamation, we read that Jesus took Himself to a private place to pray. His apostles meanwhile returned to the ship to begin a journey back to Capernaum. Night was falling, Jesus had not appeared, and the sea looked as if it was picking up. It seems that by now these, no doubt rather less than intrepid sailors, determined that they should begin the journey, either deciding to leave Jesus behind, or He may have instructed them to go on ahead. They rowed out about fifteen to thirty furlongs, or three to four miles whereupon they saw "Jesus walking on the sea, and drawing nigh unto the ship: and they were afraid" (John 6:19).

There is that fear again; fear and uncertainty can block out faith and belief. In a time of personal darkness it can be difficult to hope for, let alone see, the light. Then, the satisfying, fear-quelling words, "It is I; be not afraid" (John 6:20).

Is that not a wonderfully reassuring promise, invitation, and expression of consolation?

Most of us do experience times of personal distress, sometimes very long periods of personal fear, anxiety, and even despair. We languish in our sphere of darkness, attempting to personally cope with inner turmoil, mental strain, and physical pain. Although family, friends, Church leaders, and even doctors attempt to offer help, and sometimes do, we nevertheless can feel that we are stuck in a corner facing a troubled personal world and pleading, "Where can I get relief? Is there no end to my distress? Is peace to elude me evermore?"

President Thomas S. Monson, while serving as the First Counselor in the First Presidency of the Church, taught, "World peace, though a lofty goal, is but an outgrowth of the personal peace each individual seeks to attain. I refer not to the peace promoted by man, but peace as promised of God. I speak of peace in our homes, peace in our hearts, even peace in our lives. Peace after the way of man is perishable. Peace after the manner of God will prevail."[120]

President Monson continued,

> We find it comforting and satisfying to communicate with our Heavenly Father through prayer, that path to spiritual power—even a passport to peace. We are reminded of His Beloved Son, the Prince of Peace, that pioneer who literally showed the way for others to follow. His divine plan can save us from the Babylons of sin, complacency, and error. His example points the way. When faced with temptation, He shunned it. When offered the world, He declined it. When asked for His life, He gave it.[121]

In every respect, the Savior is the epitome of peace, the fountain of peace which comes forth as living water, the sustaining and nourishing power of peace that comes from partaking of the Bread of Life. As Paul testified, "And the peace of God, which passeth all understanding, shall keep your hearts and minds through Christ Jesus" (Philippians 4:7).

We can overcome fear with faith and peace as we reflect on the Savior's unequivocal statements of love, peace, and compassion:

"I will come and heal him." Such was not just the promise made to the centurion in behalf of his servant, it is also a promise that He makes to each one of us. At times of extremity, we can hear Him say, "I will come and heal [you]."

"It is I; be not afraid." A focus on the life and atoning mission of the Savior, and of the redemption—now and in the hereafter—from all earthly woes and sorrows, can move us to the full realization of His loving promise, "It is I; be not afraid."

"Peace, be still." This seems to me to be more of a command than a blessing or promise. As did He, we can say to the boisterous condition of our own lives, "Peace, be still." This power is ours as we turn ourselves over completely and unreservedly to Him who is the Prince of Peace.

Listen! Hear His voice! "Peace, be still."

Epilogue

"Men can only obtain permanent peace
by following after righteousness,
by being governed by the principles of truth,
by associating themselves with God our Heavenly Father,
by acknowledging His hand,
and by submitting to His law,
to His rule, to His dominion, and to His authority."

—George Q. Cannon, *Journal of Discourses*, 25:284

Notes

1. Joseph Fielding Smith, *Take Heed to Yourselves!* (Salt Lake City: Deseret Book, 1971), 364.

2. Joseph Fielding Smith, *Doctrines of Salvation*, Comp. Bruce R. McConkie (Salt Lake City: Bookcraft, 1954–6), 2:94–95.

3. Bruce R. McConkie, *Doctrines of Salvation* (Salt Lake City: Book-craft, 1954–6), 2:94–95.

4. Heber J. Grant, *Conference Report*, Oct 1899, 18.

5. George Q. Cannon, *Gospel Truth*, Jerreld L. Newquist (Salt Lake City: Deseret Book 1957), 1:20.

6. Marion G. Romney, "Guidance of the Holy Spirit." *Ensign*, Jan. 1980, 5.

7. Marion G. Romney, "Seek the Spirit." *Conference Report*, Oct 1961, 60–61.

8. George Q. Cannon, *Gospel Truth,* Jerreld L. Newquist (Salt Lake City, Deseret Book, 1957), 1:182.

9. Joseph F. Smith, *Conference Report*, Oct. 1903, 86.

10. "The Impossible Dream," *Man of LaMancha*, 1972. Music by Mitch Leigh; Lyrics by Joe Darlon.

11. Spencer W. Kimball, "When the World Will Be Converted." *Ensign*, Oct. 1974.

12. Spencer W. Kimball, "When the World Will Be Converted." *Ensign*, Oct. 1974.

13. George Q. Cannon, "The Logan Temple." *Millennial Star*, Nov. 1877, 743.

14. Heber J. Grant, J. Reuben Clark, David O. McKay, "Christmas Greetings from the First Presidency." *Deseret News*, 14 Dec 1949, Church Section, 2.

15. Vince Gill "Let there be Peace on Earth." see www.lyricsmode .com/lyrics/v/vince.gill/let_there_be_peace_on_earth.html

16. Cecil Spring-Rice, "I Vow to Thee My Country." See en.wikipedia .org/wiki/I_vow_to_thee,_my_country

17. Ezra Taft Benson, "Born of God." *Ensign,* Nov. 1985.

18. David O. McKay, "Gospel Ideals." *Improvement Era,* 1953, 292.

19. Wikipedia, "Religious War." http://en.wikipedia.org/wiki/Religious_war, accessed June 19, 2013.

20. Frederic Farrar, *The Life of Christ* (Cassell: London:1901), 2.

21. James R. Clark, comp. *Messages of the First Presidency of The Church of Jesus Christ of Latter-day Saints.* 6 vols. (Salt Lake City: Bookcraft 1965–75), 6. 189.

22. Bruce R. McConkie, *Mormon Doctrine*, Second Edition, Bookcraft, 1966, 74. A summary of this teaching can be found in the Bible Dictionary, in the LDS Edition of the Bible, (p. 614).

23. David O. McKay, *Pathway to Happiness*, comp. Llewelyn R. McKay (Salt Lake City: Bookcraft, 1967), 136–37.

24. Joseph F. Smith "The Great War." *Improvement Era,* Sep. 1914, 1075.

25. David S. Baxter, *A Perfect Brightness of Hope,* (Salt Lake City: Deseret Book, 2012).

26. Francis M. Lyman, *Conference Report*, Oct. 1899, 34.

27. Marion G. Romney, *Conferece Report*, Apr. 1974, 134.

28. Spencer W. Kimball, *The Miracle of Forgiveness* (Salt Lake City: Bookcraft, 1969), 282–4.

29. Ibid.

30. Ibid.

31. Ibid.

32. N. Eldon Tanner *Conference Report*, Apr. 1974, 76.

33. Thomas S. Monson, "School Thy Feelings, O My Brother." *Conference Report*, Oct. 2009, 64–65.

34. James E. Faust, "The Healing Power of Forgiveness." *Conference Report*, Apr. 2007.

35. George Q. Cannon, *Journal of Discourses*, 22:245.

36. J. Reuben Clark, *Behold the Lamb of God, (*Salt Lake City: Deseret Book. 1962), 131–2.

37. George Q. Cannon, *Journal of Discourses,* 22:103.
38. John Taylor, "Legitimacy and Illegitimacy." *Journal of Discourses,* 1:228.
39. Ibid.
40. Joseph B. Wirthlin, "Dikes versus Living Water." *Ensign,* Nov. 1976, 28.
41. Douglas Malloch, "Good Timber."
42. Boyd K. Packer, *Conference Report,* Apr 1978, 139–40.
43. Barbie Nadeau, "Europe's White Widows." *Newsweek,* June 25, 2012, 34–37.
44. Boyd K. Packer, "The Atonement." *Ensign,* Nov. 2012, 75–78.
45. Alexandre Dumas, *The Count of Monte Cristo* (New York: Everyman's Library, 2009), 150.
46. Neal A. Maxwell, *Notwithstanding My Weakness* (Salt Lake City: Deseret Book, 1981), 67-68.
47. Quoted in Spencer W. Kimball, *Faith Precedes the Miracle,* (Salt Lake City: Deseret Book, 2001), 98.
48. David S. Baxter, "Faith, Fortitude, Fulfillment: A Message To Single Parents." *Ensign,* May 2012, 38.
49. Personal correspondence to author. Used by permission.
50. *Preach My Gospel: A Guide to Missionary Service* (Salt Lake City: The Church of Jesus Christ of Latter-day Saints, 2004), 52. This is an abridged version of the chapter "Leaving Adversity Behind" was published in the Dec. 2012, *Ensign.* (Baxter, *Ensign,* Dcc 2012, 24–26).
51. Boyd K. Packer, *Conference Report,* Oct. 1975, 147.
52. William Wordsworth, "Ode: Intimations of Immortality from 'Recollections of Early Childhood.'" *The Best Poems of English Language: From Chaucer Through Frost.* By Herold Bloom (New York: Harper Collins, 2004), 323.
53. Ibid., 325.
54. Orson F. Whitney, "We Walk by Faith." *Improvement Era,* May 1916, 608–9.
55. Rupert Brooke, "The Soldier." *The Oxford Book of Twentieth Century Verse* (Suffolk, England: Oxford University Press), 69.
56. Spencer W. Kimball, *The Teachings of Spencer W. Kimball* (Salt Lake City: Bookcraft 1982), 45.
57. Bruce R. McConkie, *Conference Report,* Oct. 1976, 158–9.

58. Brigham Young, *Journal of Discourses.* 3:368–9. See also *Teachings of the Presidents of the Church*: *Brigham Young* (Salt Lake City: Church of Jesus Christ of Latter-day Saints), 279; *Gospel Principles* (Salt Lake City: Church of Jesus Christ of Latter-day Saints), 241–2.

59. Parley P. Pratt, *Key to the Science of Theology,* (Liverpool, England: Albert Carrington, 1877), 132–3.

60. Joseph F. Smith, *Gospel Doctrine,* 5th Ed. (Salt Lake City: Deseret Book, 1939), 440.

61. Brigham Young, *Journal of Discourses.* 8:10.

62. Lorenzo Snow, *Millennial Star,* Jan. 22, 1894, 50.

63. Joseph F. Smith, "Funeral Discourse." *Journal of Discourses.* 22:351.

64. Harold B. Lee, *The Teachings of Harold B. Lee* (Salt Lake City: Bookcraft, 1996), 414–5.

65. *Handbook 2: Administering the Church* (Salkt Lake City: The Church of Jesus Christ of Latter-day Saints, 2010), 197.

66. Joseph Smith, *History of the Church.* 4:554.

67. Spencer W. Kimball, *Faith Precedes the Miracle* (Salt Lake City: Deseret Book, 1993), 101.

68. Joseph F. Smith, *Teachings of the Prophet Joseph Smith* (Salt Lake City: Deseret Book), 196–7.

69. Joseph Fielding Smith, *Doctrines of Salvation, 2:54.* "The Salvation of Little Children." *Ensign,* Apr. 1977, 5.

70. Joseph F. Smith, *Gospel Doctrine* (Salt Lake City: Deseret Book, 1939), 455–6.

71. Spencer W. Kimball, "Tragedy or Destiny." *Improvement Era,* Mar. 1966, 180, 210.

72. Joseph F. Smith, *Gospel Doctrine* (Salt Lake City: Deseret Book, 1939), 65.

73. "How Great the Wisdom and the Love," *Hymns,* no. 195.

74. "He is Risen!" *Hymns, no.* 199.

75. George Q. Cannon, *Millenial Star* 39, 12 Nov. 1877, 743.

76. L. Tom Perry, "As Now We Take the Sacrament." *Ensign,* May 2006, 39–42.

77. Russell M. Nelson, "Worshipping at Sacrament Meeting." *Ensign* Aug 2004, 24–28 (this entire article is recommended to the reader).

78. Joseph F. Smith, "The Sacrament of the Lord's Supper." *Journal of Discourses.* 15:324.

79. "Prayer is the Soul's Sincere Desire," *Hymns,* no. 145.

80. Richter, Johann (also Jean Paul Richter), *Forty Thousand Quotations: Prose and Poetical*, comp. by Charles Noel Douglas. (New York: Halcyon House, 1917; Bartleby.com) www.bartleby .com/348/1110.html#4

81. Marion G. Romney, *Conference Report*, Oct. 1964, 51.

82. Joseph Fielding Smith, *Answers to Gospel Questions* Vol.3 (Salt Lake City: Deseret Book, 2009), 3–5.

83. "Secret Prayer," *Hymns,* no. 144.

84. "Come, Come, Ye Saints," *Hymns,* no. 30.

85. For a fuller description of these circumstances, see David S. Baxter, *A Perfect Brightness of Hope* (Salt Lake City: Deseret Book, 2011).

86. Andrew D. Olsen, *Price We Paid* (Salt Lake City: Deseret Book, 2006), 422–5

87. James E. Faust, "Faith in Every Footstep: The Epic Pioneer Journey." *Ensign,* May 1997, 63. See also James E. Faust, "The Refiner's Fire." *Ensign,* May 1979, 53.

88. David O. McKay, "Faith in Christ—The World's Greatest Need." *Improvement Era*, Jan. 1944, 62.

89. Neal A. Maxwell, "Notwithstanding My Weakness." *Ensign,* Nov. 1976, 13.

90. Ezra Taft Benson, "Do Not Despair." *Ensign,* Nov. 1974, 67.

91. Truman G. Madsen, *The Presidents of the Church* (Salt Lake City: Deseret Book, 2004), 348.

92. Gordon B. Hinckley, *Conference Report*, Apr. 1998, 68.

93. Heber J. Grant, *Gospel Standards: Selections from the Sermons and Writings of Heber J. Grant*, Comp. G. Homer Durham (Salt Lake City: Deseret Book, 1941), 111.

94. Gordon B. Hinckley, *Conference Report*, Oct 1998, 71–72.

95. See Wikipedia.org/wiki/Serenity_Prayer for origins and variations.

96. Harold B. Lee, *The Teachings of Harold B. Lee*, (Salt Lake City: Bookcraft, 1996), 82.

97. Personal recollections.

98. Dallin H. Oaks, published reference unknown.

99. George Q. Cannon, *Gospel Truth*, Comp. Jereld L. Newquist (Salt Lake City: Deseret Book, 1957), 2:313.

100. Spencer W. Kimball, *The Teachings of Spencer W. Kimball* (Salt Lake City: Bookcraft, 1982), 362.

101. George Q. Cannon, *Gospel Truth*, Comp. Jereld L. Newquist (Salt Lake City: Deseret Book, 1957), 2:312.

102. Joseph F. Smith, *Gospel Doctrine*, 5th Ed (Salt Lake City: Deseret Book, 1939), 235–6.

103. www.ameliaearhart.com/about/quotes.html

104. Heber J. Grant, "Work and Keep your Promises." *Improvement Era*, Jan. 1900, 195.

105. Spencer W. Kimball, "Train Up a Child." *Ensign*, Apr. 1978, web.

106. David O. McKay, "Gospel Ideals," *Improvement Era*, 1953, 487.

107. David O. McKay, *Conference Report*, Apr. 1935, 113.

108. "The Family: A Proclamation to the World." The First Presidency and Council of the Twelve Apostles of The Church of Jesus Christ of Latter-day Saints, Sep 27, 1995.

109. David O. McKay, *Conference Report*, Oct 1939, 149.

110. David O. McKay, *Conference Report*, Oct 1967, 149.

111. Gordon B. Hinckley, *Conference Report*, Oct 1991, 70–71.

112. Ibid., 70.

113. Ibid., 71.

114. Spencer W. Kimball, "Living the Gospel in the Home." *Ensign,* May 1978, 101.

115. M. Russell Ballard, "O, Be Wise." *Conference Report*, Oct. 2006, 16–17.

116. Ibid., 17–19.

117. L. Z. Granderson, "Kid, you are not Special." CNN.com, June 12, 2012. see also, David McCullough Jr. "You're Not Special." *Newsweek,* June 25, 26–27.

118. Rudyard Kipling, "If." *The Oxford Book of Twentieth Century Verse* (Suffolk, England: Oxford University Press, 1973), 69.

119. Frederic Farrar, *The Life of Christ* (London: Cassell, 1901), 149.

120. Thomas S. Monson, "Finding Peace." *Ensign*, Mar. 2004.

121. Ibid.

About the Author

David Baxter was born in Stirling, Scotland, and became a General Authority of The Church of Jesus Christ of Latter-day Saints in 2006. He previously worked in senior leadership roles in the telecommunications industry and on the boards of various UK government agencies and holds a bachelor of science in economics. In his Church service, he has been a bishop, a stake president, a member of a mission presidency, and an Area Seventy, and he is currently a member of the First Quorum of the Seventy. He has served in Church Area Presidencies in Europe and the Pacific. His early home life was traumatic and disrupted, and in 2009 he underwent surgery to remove two brain tumors. He and his wife, Dianne, are the parents of four children and the grandparents of nine grandchildren.